Self-Empowerment

Getting What You Want from Life

Revised Edition

Sam R. Lloyd and
Tina Berthelot

A Fifty-Minute™ Series Book

This Fifty-Minute™ book is designed to be "read with a pencil." It is an excellent workbook for self-study as well as classroom learning. All material is copyright-protected and cannot be duplicated without permission from the publisher. *Therefore, be sure to order a copy for every training participant by contacting:*

1-800-442-7477

Menlo Park, CA
CrispLearning.com

Self-Empowerment

Getting What You Want from Life

Revised Edition

**Sam R. Lloyd and
Tina Berthelot**

CREDITS:
Senior Editor: **Debbie Woodbury**
Editor: **Ann Gosch**
Assistant Editor: **Genevieve Del Rosario**
Production Manager: **Judy Petry**
Design: **Nicole Phillips**
Production Artist: **Zach Hooker**
Cartoonist: **Ralph Mapson**

© 1992, 2003 Crisp Publications, Inc.
Printed in the United States of America by Von Hoffmann Graphics, Inc.

CrispLearning.com

02 03 04   10 9 8 7 6 5 4 3 2

Library of Congress Catalog Card Number 2001095524
Lloyd, Sam R. and Tina Berthelot
Self-Empowerment
ISBN 1-56052-649-1

Learning Objectives For:

SELF-EMPOWERMENT

The objectives for *Self-Empowerment, Revised Edition,* are listed below. They have been developed to guide you, the reader, to the core issues covered in this book.

THE OBJECTIVES OF THIS BOOK ARE:

❑ 1) To explain the terminology and principles of empowerment

❑ 2) To present techniques for empowering self and others

❑ 3) To increase your personal success with proven tools and techniques

ASSESSING YOUR PROGRESS

In addition to the learning objectives, Crisp Learning has developed an **assessment** that covers the fundamental information presented in this book. A 25-item, multiple-choice and true-false questionnaire allows the reader to evaluate his or her comprehension of the subject matter. To buy the assessment and answer key, go to www.CrispLearning.com and search on the book title, or call 1-800-442-7477.

Assessments should not be used in any employee selection process.

About the Authors

Sam R. Lloyd is president of SuccessSystems, Inc., an international training and consulting firm based in Boulder, Colorado. Sam has worked with organizations for over 25 years providing training for a wide variety of individual and organizational needs. Sam served for 10 years as a university faculty member and administrator, and has a background in sales, sales training, and supervision in the insurance industry. Besides heading SuccessSystems for 20 years, Sam has also completed all coursework for his Ph.D. in Organizational Behavior. In addition to *Self-Empowerment,* Sam is the author of *Developing Positive Assertiveness* and *Accountability,* both by Crisp Publications.

Tina Berthelot is vice president and co-owner of SuccessSystems, Inc. Tina has worked with thousands of people in all kinds of organizations during the 17 years she has been part of SuccessSystems. Her specialty is training to improve the personal and interpersonal effectiveness of her participants. She has received outstanding ratings from those she has taught, including clients from Bristol-Myers Squibb, Hewlett-Packard, StorageTek, and the county of San Bernardino, California.

How to Use This Book

This *Fifty-Minute™ Series Book* is a unique, user-friendly product. As you read through the material, you will quickly experience the interactive nature of the book. There are numerous exercises, real-world case studies, and examples that invite your opinion, as well as checklists, tips, and concise summaries that reinforce your understanding of the concepts presented.

A Crisp Learning *Fifty-Minute™ Book* can be used in variety of ways. Individual self-study is one of the most common. However, many organizations use *Fifty-Minute* books for pre-study before a classroom training session. Other organizations use the books as a part of a systemwide learning program—supported by video and other media based on the content in the books. Still others work with Crisp Learning to customize the material to meet their specific needs and reflect their culture. Regardless of how it is used, we hope you will join the more than 20 million satisfied learners worldwide who have completed a *Fifty-Minute Book.*

Preface

Originally, our decision to write this book sprang from the interest in the idea of empowering others, and our experience as training consultants that only self-empowered people were very good at empowering others. We have learned that many organizations have used this book to help people learn about being more accountable for their own decisions and actions as well as being more effective with other people.

In revising this book, we have retained the original content that was designed to help you, the reader, improve your personal effectiveness and success by building your self-esteem and by improving your goal-setting, planning, and skills for interacting with others. We also have added the objective of helping you to be the kind of person who is comfortably accountable for your own choices and behaviors. Workers who demonstrate competence, loyalty, and a positive attitude are the most likely to be selected for empowerment by their managers. Managers expect employees at all levels to be accountable for their decisions and actions, and self-empowered employees are most likely to live up to that expectation.

Our new book, *Accountability: Managing for Maximum Results,* is designed to help managers work with their employees to produce this outcome. (Be sure your manager reads it!) In this book you will learn how to become self-empowered and accountable. To get the best results it is important for you to complete each exercise, practice the recommended techniques, and immediately start the process of self-empowerment. We wish you success!

Sam R. Lloyd

Tina Berthelot

Contents

Part 4: Management Skills

Part 5: Your Personal Development Program

Appendix

P A R T 1

The Need for Self-Empowerment

Trusting Others to Act Responsibly

Truly excellent organizations accomplish their goals and achieve success through the efforts of the people who make up the organization—but only when those people have the freedom to think and act, to question policies and procedures that interfere with quality or service, and to experiment and innovate. Thus, a key element in creating excellence is for people throughout the organization to feel empowered.

For people to feel empowered, they must:

➤ Have the authority to make decisions and to act without having to get approval each time

➤ Feel free to use their own intelligence, experience, intuition, and creativity to help the organization improve and succeed

➤ Be kept informed and involved in the organization's operations

➤ Believe their managers listen to and use their ideas

In turn, managers expect those they have empowered to use the power responsibly and to be accountable for their decisions and actions. So it quickly becomes obvious that empowerment requires mutual trust. Without trust in employees' abilities, intelligence, loyalty, and motivation, a manager will have great difficulty truly empowering them. A parent who lacks trust will be reluctant to allow children the freedom to go where they want, when they want, and with whom they choose.

Establishing Mutual Trust

If your manager seems reluctant to empower you fully, you can help by making it easier for your manager to trust in you and your abilities. What does it take for people to trust each other?

_____

_____

_____

If you want to help someone trust you more, you can demonstrate your trustworthiness to that person in the following ways:

➤ Keep your commitments.

➤ Tell the truth (even when it might be embarrassing).

➤ Be accountable for your decisions and actions.

➤ Avoid participating in gossip.

➤ Be consistently assertive with people.*

Building Trust through Confidence

People with the highest self-esteem find it easiest to trust others. And a major influence on self-empowerment, as you will learn in Part 2, is self-esteem. Self-empowered people find it easier to trust because their self-esteem and confidence do not depend upon the approval of others. On the other hand, those with fragile self-esteem worry about what others think of them and keep problems and feelings to themselves. They fear trusting others, and this fear diminishes their self-empowerment.

---

* *To learn more about assertiveness, read* Developing Positive Assertiveness *by Sam R. Lloyd, Crisp Publications.*

EVALUATE YOUR TRUST LEVEL

Evaluate yourself with the inventory below. Check (✔) each statement you believe is true.

1. ____ If you want something done right, do it yourself.

2. ____ Most people enjoy personal achievements and want to do well.

3. ____ When the cat is away, the mice will play.

4. ____ I am comfortable letting people do things their own way.

5. ____ I share my problems and feelings with at least a few people regularly.

6. ____ I worry when I don't know the status of projects.

7. ____ You just can't get good workers anymore.

8. ____ I prefer to receive frequent progress reports—daily would be ideal.

9. ____ I want employees to tell me about problems as soon as they occur.

10. ____ I frequently ask others for ideas about problems.

11. ____ It's dangerous to confide in most people because they can't keep secrets.

12. ____ A real leader makes decisions, gives clear directives, and does not tolerate anyone questioning his or her decisions.

Compare your answers with the authors' suggested responses in the Appendix.

Relating Cooperatively with Others

Self-empowerment enables you to relate effectively with other people. Organizations are most effective when people function cooperatively in teams that communicate well. In the same way, families are most successful when they share and support one another. Indeed, relationships of all kinds work best when each person has the skills and commitment to keep communication open and honest.

Interpersonal Traits

Self-empowered people have the ability to maintain good relationships and interpersonal effectiveness. Take a look at the characteristics of the opposite personalities below. You'll see that Person A is willing to expend some effort to make the relationship mutually rewarding and pleasant, while Person B lacks elements of self-empowerment. Whom would you rather have as a boss? as a friend? as an employee? as a mate?

Person A	Person B
➤ Passes along information to you	➤ Keeps information to himself or herself
➤ Asks about you	➤ Limits conversation to impersonal topics
➤ Listens well and often	➤ Interrupts and does not listen
➤ Seeks your opinion	➤ Rejects your suggestions
➤ Expresses appreciation	➤ Takes you for granted
➤ Shares concerns and problems	➤ Keeps everything to himself or herself
➤ Seems to care about you	➤ Seems disinterested in you

Person B's hoarding of information is a common means of control and self-protection, a strategy that often results from a lack of self-assurance. Restricting interactions to impersonal topics and avoiding self-disclosure may result from discomfort with intimacy or from a lack of trust.

Now turn the microscope around and examine yourself. Are you more like A or B in your relationships with your boss, your employees, your friends, and your family? Think about each of those relationships separately. You may discover that you are guilty of making a half-hearted effort in at least some of your relationships.

Few people excel at all aspects of relationships, but self-empowered people do better than most!

CASE STUDY: Interpersonal Failing Leads to Firing

Robert was an excellent student and athlete in college. Everyone expected him to have a successful career. By the time he was 30, those who had known him in his younger years were puzzled. Robert had changed employers three times since graduation, telling others that each move was part of his plan for moving up in the business world.

His old acquaintances became aware that Robert seemed angry and stressed most of the time. He frequently complained about his boss and his employees. No one was surprised when he announced that he had been fired and was looking for another job. Several months passed and Robert was unsuccessful in his job search.

In desperation, Robert applied for a position in a company where an old classmate, Paul, worked as the human resources manager. Paul was surprised to see Robert's application because the position was lower in responsibility and salary than Robert's past employment. When he checked with previous employers, a pattern emerged. Each said positive things about Robert's decision-making and motivation but also suggested that he could use some help with his ability to deal with people.

During the interviews and assessment process, Paul noticed that Robert made disparaging remarks about his former employers and employees. For this reason, Paul chose another candidate—one with a record of good relationships with people and who impressed everyone with his good communication skills.

Check (✔) the characteristics Robert seemed to lack:

❑ **Motivation** ❑ **Trust**

❑ **Intelligence** ❑ **Enthusiasm**

❑ **Experience** ❑ **Decision-making skills**

❑ **Interpersonal skills** ❑ **Confidence**

Compare your answers to the authors' comments in the Appendix.

Achieving Personal Success

As you become more self-empowered, you will have the tools and skills for creating more successes in your life. People have differing ideas about success.

How do you define success? Write a brief definition below.

_____

_____

_____

_____

_____

Some people think of success in relation to money, or accomplishments, or love and happiness. But let's define success this way: setting goals and achieving them. Success is a continuous experience and not some remote destination to be reached someday. No matter what your goals are—money, love, power, fame, and so on—when you achieve your goals, you achieve success.

Being self-empowered requires having clearly defined goals based on your own values and having the persistence and abilities to achieve your goals. Later in this book you will learn the steps for defining achievable goals as part of your personal development plan. For now, though, turn to the next section to learn about building your self-esteem in your journey to self-empowerment.

Building Blocks of Self-Empowerment

Understanding Self-Esteem

A self-empowered person is one with high self-esteem. It is difficult to imagine how someone without self-respect and self-confidence could ever be considered self-empowered. Building your self-esteem is a major step in becoming self-empowered.

What is self-esteem? In the following exercise, circle **T** for true or **F** for false.

T F Self-esteem can vary depending upon situations, events, health, and so on.

T F Self-esteem is a blend of internal confidence and external achievements.

T F Self-esteem is something anyone can increase and maintain at a higher level.

T F Self-esteem is affected by early life experiences.

T F Your self-esteem is reflected in your judgments of yourself.

T F Our beliefs and values can make it difficult to maintain high self-esteem.

If you marked all of the items true, you understand that self-esteem varies in each person and is shaped and affected by many elements.

To better understand how self-esteem is developed, let's break it down into three main components:

> **Self-image**

> **Self-talk**

> **Self-determination**

When you understand how each of these components operates and how to change each, you will be able to build your own self-esteem. This may be the most important accomplishment for becoming a self-empowered person.

Assessing Self-Image

If you were asked to describe your self-image, you might have a difficult time putting into words how you see yourself. You probably do not have a day-to-day awareness of your self-image, but you do see yourself in a certain way and it affects how you live every day. Your self-image affects:

➤ How you interpret what people say and do

➤ How you choose to act in a situation

➤ How you feel about yourself and others

Your self-image is a constant influence on your perceptions of yourself, others, and life in general.

TAKING A SELF-IMAGE INVENTORY

Evaluate your own self-image. In the space below, list your strengths or positive characteristics and your weaknesses or negative characteristics.

Strengths	Weaknesses
_____	_____
_____	_____
_____	_____
_____	_____
_____	_____
_____	_____
_____	_____
_____	_____
_____	_____
_____	_____
_____	_____

Which did you find easier to identify—your strengths or your weaknesses? Many people tend to be more aware of their faults than their positive qualities. If that is true for you, then you must learn to give yourself credit for your strengths and to break the habit of giving more weight to your weaknesses.

Did you list an equal number of strengths and weaknesses? The same number of spaces was provided for each, but you may have thought of more in one category than the other. If you listed more negative characteristics than positives, start paying more attention to your positive attributes and add new strengths to your list as you work through this book and complete other self-improvement projects.

Rethinking Negative Self-Judgments

Some personal traits you listed as weaknesses or negative characteristics can be evaluated differently if you change your perspective. Other people may view as an endearing quality something you see as a fault or undesirable trait. We often apply a negative label to ourselves, using an excessively harsh judgment that may be viewed more positively by a more objective observer.

We can look at ourselves from a different perspective by considering other ways to describe the same characteristic with more realistic or forgiving words. Examine the list below and write a more positive description of the same quality in the space provided.

Negative Trait		Positive Version
lazy	➜	_____
shy	➜	_____
loud	➜	_____
fat	➜	_____

Was that difficult? Did you figure out a way to describe the negative traits in a more forgiving, more positive manner? Alternatives for the list above could include the following:

lazy = *laid-back, minimalist, energy-conserving*

shy = *quiet, retiring, unobtrusive*

loud = *enthusiastic, exuberant, vocal*

fat = *large, robust, hefty*

Now return to your list of personal negative characteristics and do the same with your own negative self-judgments. Figure out a way to describe those traits with less severe, more accepting words.

This is not to say you should engage in self-deception, but to allow yourself to feel better about yourself by being less critical of your traits. You may have behaviors that still need to be changed, and these will be addressed later in this book.

Embracing Positive Self-Talk

Do you talk to yourself? ❑ Yes ❑ No

You should have answered yes because everyone does, and with some frequency. It is a normal practice. Some people do it aloud, and some even have two-way conversations.

The big question is: *How* do you talk with yourself? Do you say positive, supporting things, or do you berate yourself and say disapproving things? If you habitually say negative things to yourself, you are keeping your self-esteem at a lower level than it could be.

The Problem with Self-Criticism

Imagine how you would feel if you had a hypercritical boss telling you every day how badly you were doing and how you would never improve. Imagine what it would be like to have a disapproving parent with you to chastise you any time you made a mistake, broke a rule, or forgot something.

That is exactly what many of us do to ourselves with negative self-talk. Some who have studied this aspect of human behavior have estimated that as much as 80% of the average person's self-talk is negative. That much daily disapproval could erode anyone's self-esteem.

Read the examples below and check (✔) any that are similar to statements you have said to yourself.

❑ *"I can't believe I missed my exit! Boy, am I stupid!"*

❑ *"I hope I don't forget what I'm supposed to say. I don't want to make a fool of myself."*

❑ *"I can't believe I just said that. I'm always putting my foot in my mouth!"*

❑ *"Slow, slow! I am so darned slow."*

❑ *"You did it again, dummy! Don't you ever learn?"*

❑ *"Oh no! I'm such a klutz!"*

❑ *"I just can't figure it out. I've never been any good at this."*

Do these sound familiar? Almost all people do this to themselves. Become aware and acknowledge how often you do this and what your most frequent self-denigrating remarks are. This is the first step toward changing this habit into a self-empowering technique.

Replacing Self-Criticism with Constructive Comments

Many of the negative labels we give ourselves were applied to us early in life by other people. As small children we heard adults saying that we were this or that, and we believed them. Some of the disapproving messages we heard became part of our self-image and perceptions of reality.

The point is not to become angry with the adults who were early influences in your life. Your challenge now is to break free of such limits on your self-esteem. Everyone carries a load of early labels and self-defeating habits. Becoming self-empowered means lightening that load.

Here are some load-lightening guidelines. When you hear yourself saying—internally or aloud—such expressions as those in the left-hand list, learn to say instead something like the kinder examples in the right-hand list.

Old Self-Talk	New Self-Talk
"I'm so clumsy!"	"Oops, I spilled my coffee."
"Boy, that was stupid."	"I wasn't paying attention—stay alert."
"What if they don't like my idea?"	"This is a good idea—I hope they like it."
"I can't go on that trip until I get caught up at work."	"I want to go, and the break from work will do me good."
"I should visit my parents."	"I could visit my parents, but it's okay to go skiing if I want."
"I'll never get the hang of this."	"Calm down, think clearly—you can do it."

It will take practice to change your self-talk from restricting your self-empowerment to encouraging it. By sticking with your commitment, keeping a journal of negative self-talk, and practicing more positive and energizing self-talk, you will experience an exciting new feeling of power.

MY SELF-CRITICISM

Write below the negative self-talk you use regularly. Take your time and recall recent situations in which you failed to live up to your own expectations.

_____

_____

_____

_____

_____

_____

_____

_____

_____

_____

If you think of more as you proceed, turn back to this page and add them to this list. Keep a journal for the next few weeks. Each day record your self-talk or keep a total of the negative and positive self-talk each day. Until you become aware of your self-talk, you will be unable to change it into supportive and encouraging messages.

Read some of the messages you identified with in our list on page 17 and some of the ones you wrote in the self-criticism exercise above. Imagine saying those things to a valued employee or a friend or family member. You might think, "Heavens, I would never say that to them!"

Isn't it interesting that we say such things to ourselves? You can learn to be as considerate of yourself as you are of others and replace negative self-talk with constructive criticism.

Engaging in Self-Determination

A final part of building self-esteem is becoming more self-determined. What does self-determination mean?

Self-determined people are goal-directed with a clear understanding of what they want from life. And they go about making sure they get it. Obviously, such people must have high self-esteem and positive expectations to accomplish their goals. They see themselves as deserving of what they want and capable of achieving whatever they set out to do.

The following case study will help you understand self-determination.

CASE STUDY: Lamenting Life Lost

Jack is a sales manager who is within six months of retiring from his lifelong employment in sales. He talks with a peer over lunch. "It's hard to believe I'll be retiring in another six months." His friend asks, "Are you looking forward to it, Jack?"

"You bet I am! Maybe now I'll have some time to do things I've always wanted to do. I've enjoyed my work but it demanded so much of my time and energy that I never seemed to find time to travel or do a lot of other things. I mean, Fran and I had a good life, but so many things seemed to pass us by. We intended to do more fun things but just never seemed to be able to find the time. Maybe now we can."

The friend comments, "Well, you'll certainly have the time now!" To which Jack responds, "Yeah, but I'm not sure that my retirement income will be enough for us to afford much beyond the basics. Inflation has been so bad that we're not going to be as comfortable as I had hoped."

See the authors' comments to this case study in the Appendix.

HOW SELF-DETERMINED ARE YOU?

Rate yourself on the following items, between 1 if you are weak in that area and 5 if you are strong. Be honest. Add up all your circled numbers at the end of the exercise to get your total score.

	Weak			Strong	
I set specific goals at least annually.	1	2	3	4	5
I have clear five-year goals and retirement goals.	1	2	3	4	5
I discuss my values and wants with family or friends.	1	2	3	4	5
I use a daily planner or to-do list.	1	2	3	4	5
I plan my leisure time to make sure I enjoy it.	1	2	3	4	5
I enjoy my work and get real satisfaction from it.	1	2	3	4	5
I feel that I am in charge of my life.	1	2	3	4	5
I accomplish most of my goals.	1	2	3	4	5
I manage money well.	1	2	3	4	5
I feel very satisfied with how my life is going.	1	2	3	4	5
I have successful personal relationships.	1	2	3	4	5
I have a good balance of work, play, and family.	1	2	3	4	5

TOTAL SCORE

_____

If you scored in the range of:

45–60 You are doing a very good job of determining your life.

25–44 You are among the great majority who manage fairly well but could get more satisfaction from life by improving your self-determination.

12–24 You have been letting life happen to you, and you will benefit greatly from completing this book and mastering the ideas and techniques.

Expecting Positive Outcomes

A fascinating aspect of self-empowerment is the role played by a person's expectations and attitudes, a phenomenon known as *self-fulfilling prophecy*. People see what they expect to see, experience what they expect to experience, achieve what they expect to achieve, and fail when they expect to fail.

Self-Fulfilling Prophecy at Work

Proof of the self-fulfilling prophecy's influence on outcomes in organizations was evident as long ago as 1890. The U.S. Census Bureau installed new tabulating machines that required census workers to learn new skills that were thought to be difficult. The workers were told that after some practice they would be able to punch about 550 cards a day and that processing more than that number might be harmful to their psychological health. As you might expect, after two weeks they were processing a little over 500 cards a day and reporting stress symptoms when they exceeded that number.

Additional clerks were hired later to operate the same machines, but were told nothing about limits on the productivity rate. After only three days, the new workers were processing over 2,000 cards a day with no ill effects. The original workers believed they could produce only 550 cards, and that is what they did. The new workers had no limited expectations and produced at a much higher rate.

This example dramatically demonstrates how much we can accomplish when we start with positive expectations. And it suggests what a positive influence we can be for others when we have positive expectations of them.

CASE STUDY: Expectations and Outcomes

Terry, Pat, and Connie work in the same company, and all are supervisors. Their performance is being scrutinized carefully by upper management to decide who is the best candidate for promotion to middle management.

Terry is known as a hard worker who often comes early and stays late. She speaks frequently about having to work hard and shows signs of worry and stress. When her department's output is examined, the productivity is comparable to the other departments. The management team discovers that several employees have complained about the pressure in this department.

Pat has been with the company longer than the others and has been passed over before when promotion was considered. Pat's reputation is hampered by a persistent pessimism. Others joke about his stock reactions, which are "That will never work" and "If it ain't broke, don't fix it." Pat's department has the highest turnover and the lowest productivity.

Connie is a relaxed, efficient person who rarely comes early or stays late. Connie spends a lot of time moving about her department talking with employees. Her file has no grievances in it, and her productivity and turnover figures are the best of the three. The management team is impressed with how Connie gets so much accomplished without seeming to work hard at all.

Do you agree that Connie seems to be the best candidate? ❑ Yes ❑ No

If Connie is the star of this trio, what are her most important differences?

_____

_____

Compare your answers to the authors' comments in the Appendix.

WHAT DO YOU EXPECT?

Think of how your expectations affect your actual experience. When you contemplate a new challenge, do you expect an easy victory or a struggle? When you think about the party you will attend, do you anticipate having fun or being bored? Respond as spontaneously and honestly as you can to each of the following situations.

1. Your boss tells you that you will be making an important presentation to the senior management group in two days. What is your reaction? What is your mental picture?

    _____

    _____

2. Your spouse asks you to accompany him or her to the high school reunion, and you agree to go. What are your expectations?

    _____

    _____

3. You are hired to be the manager who supervises the three people described in the previous case study: Terry, Pat, and Connie. What are your expectations for each relationship?

    Terry: _____

    _____

    Pat: _____

    _____

    Connie: _____

    _____

Compare your answers with the authors' responses in the Appendix.

Recognizing Selective Perception

As you are learning, the challenge in building self-empowerment is becoming aware of attitudes and expectations and changing those that are self-defeating. This includes expectations of ourselves and of others. A part of this is the filtering process called *selective perception*. We constantly filter out many of the sights and sounds around us, allowing only a manageable amount through from our subconscious mind to our conscious awareness. This is necessary for our sanity.

A simple example of this is what happens after you purchase a new car. Don't you suddenly start noticing all of the cars on the road like yours? Those cars were there all along, of course, but you noticed them only when you changed your expectations and awareness.

The subconscious mind is a powerful influence on perceptions and behavior. Subconscious expectations and attitudes result not only in your noticing some things and not others, but also in your being sensitive to some words and not others and saying and doing some things and not others. The perceptions that we allow ourselves to be aware of are those that are consistent with our expectations and attitudes.

Self-empowered people take charge of this process by developing expectations and attitudes that prompt effective behavior and influence others in positive ways.

TRUTH OR BIAS?

To become more aware of your expectations and attitudes, be honest in identifying your thoughts on the following statements. Write an **A** in the blank if you *agree*, or **D** if you *disagree*.

1. _____ If you want something done right, do it yourself.

2. _____ Most people want to do their best and achieve good results.

3. _____ Men are better decision-makers than women are.

4. _____ Most organizations exploit people when possible.

5. _____ Some people do as little as they can get away with.

6. _____ Young people today don't appreciate the value of money.

7. _____ Women are better suited for parenting than men are.

8. _____ You don't tamper with success.

9. _____ Most people care only about themselves.

10. _____ If you want something done right, do it yourself.

11. _____ People with college degrees make better managers.

Did the statements hit a nerve or two? Did you allow yourself to answer honestly? Admitting to prejudices is difficult, but we all have them and need to recognize them.

What are the correct answers? Research substantiates some of the above statements and repudiates others, but the "right" answer is not that important for this exercise. The important point is that whatever you believe about each statement will influence your perception and actual behavior in situations related to that issue.

If you believe that men are better decision-makers than women are, you will tend to discount the thinking of women—regardless of your own sex—and give more credit to men's ideas. If you expect people to work hard and do well, they probably will. But if you expect them to give minimum effort, they probably will. Your expectations get communicated through subtle daily behaviors, and people usually respond the way you think they will.

Self-Programming for Success

The famous entrepreneur Henry Ford once said something to the effect of, "If you think you can or you think you cannot, you are always right!" He understood that we unconsciously *program* ourselves to experience life just the way we assumed it would be.

Develop and practice the habit of assuming positive outcomes by writing statements such as these on index cards or self-adhesive notes:

> *"I can learn to dance the tango."*
>
> *"I can ask my boss for a raise."*
>
> *"I can confront Bob about his late arrivals."*

Read the messages to yourself several times each day for a week or two before you take the planned action. Your chances for success are greatly improved by programming your expectations for positive outcomes.

Joel Weldon, a professional speaker, has said, "Success comes in cans, not in cannots!"

---

* *For more information on self-programming, read* Developing Positive Assertiveness *by Sam Lloyd and* Stress That Motivates *by Dru Scott, both by Crisp Publications.*

COMMUNICATING POSITIVE EXPECTATIONS

When you have positive expectations and attitudes about yourself, you feel more empowered and experience more success. When you have positive expectations of others, you act as an influence and help empower them, too. Communicating to empower involves using the *win-win* or "I'm okay–you're okay" philosophy.

Check (✔) the situations below that are "I'm okay–you're okay" or win-win examples.

___ 1. A manager says to an employee, "I'm impressed with the thoroughness of this report, Tracy. I can always depend on you to do a good job."

___ 2. When a team member arrives late for a meeting, the leader rolls his eyes and exhales loudly.

___ 3. A parent speaking to a teenager says, "Don't forget to clean your room today and don't leave your dirty clothes piled up in the corner!"

___ 4. A teacher says to a student, "You are going to learn a lot about how nature works in this section."

___ 5. Two managers are talking about their teams. One says, "Even though the people on my team are mostly new, I can tell they are going to set some records."

___ 6. An employee asks the manager, "Will you check this and give me some feedback?"

___ 7. One worker says to another, "Isn't that typical? You can always count on management to make things more difficult."

___ 8. An employee notices another struggling with a complaining customer over the telephone and offers a smile and a thumbs-up hand signal.

___ 9. A friend compliments you on your presentation, saying, "That was a super job. I could never pull that off so smoothly."

___ 10. A manager is thinking about conducting a performance review with an employee: "I don't know how to handle this one. This is going to be really tough for him to take."

Compare your answers with the authors' responses in the Appendix.

Interpersonal Skills

Communicating What You Want

We all live and work in a world full of other people, and being self-empowered means having skills for interacting effectively with these people. Even the most positive and confident person will not accomplish much without the skills to communicate and cooperate with others.

People are often stymied about what to do or say when they don't know what they want. Here are two examples in which the ability to communicate effectively is hindered by indecision. What would you recommend in each situation?

To Supervise or NOT to Supervise?

Sandra works in the finance department. She has the training and experience to qualify for a supervisory position that has opened up in her department. Sandra enjoys her current work, but lately she has been aware that she no longer feels challenged. She would like to earn more money and is seriously thinking about telling her boss that she would like to be considered for the supervisory position. Sandra is hesitating because she is not sure whether she wants the additional responsibility or if she would enjoy supervising others.

What steps do you recommend for Sandra?

_____

_____

_____

To Want Help or to Go It Alone

Martin has been working on a project that is a new challenge for him; it requires creativity and some new ways of thinking. Marsha, who has handled similar projects, has dropped by a couple of times to offer helpful suggestions. Today she pauses before leaving Martin's office and says, "Martin, I'm never sure whether you appreciate my help or not. I can't tell what you really want." Marsha leaves with a friendly wave.

Martin wonders about her comment and realizes he is not sure about his preferences. Marsha's suggestions have been useful and have helped him progress more quickly, but he is aware that he might feel better about his accomplishment if he did it without her help.

What do you think Martin needs to do?

_____

_____

_____

Did you recommend that Sandra do something to help her decide what she really wants for herself? That would be a necessary first step before she could decide what other actions to take. Did you suggest that Martin do the same thing? His friend has noticed that he is sending mixed signals, and he himself is wondering what he really wants.

Making Choices

Most of our life situations present us with options, and making choices can prove to be challenging. Self-empowered people are aware of their own values and preferences and feel comfortable with allowing their wants—rather than what might please others—to be the most important deciding factor.

Often it is easier to decide what you *do not* want. That can be a helpful first step toward identifying your wants, but it is important to become aware of what you *do* want. Knowing only what you *do not* want can lead to passivity in your dealings with others. Knowing what you *do* want and actively ensuring that you get your wants satisfied are necessary to being self-empowered.

When you have clearly defined wants and priorities you will be more confident in your decision-making, and you also will be more comfortable being accountable for the outcome of your decisions.

IDENTIFY WHAT YOU WANT

Knowing what you want in your own life is not always as easy as when examining another person's situation. A good starting point for improving your interpersonal skills is learning to identify your "want" in a situation. Practice in the following examples.

Situation	I Want
Your boss gives you a complicated assignment that must be completed by 5:00 tomorrow.	
Relatives arrive for a surprise visit expecting to stay a week.	
You were planning to eat alone and read a good book when two co-workers ask you to join them.	
Your spouse asks if you would like to join his or her after-work gathering of co-workers or meet at home later.	
You win a contest and have a choice of $200 or a mystery prize guaranteed to be worth at least $200.	

Did you discover that you had more than one want in some situations? For example, you might want advance notice from your boss or more time for completing the assignment. You might want to spend time with your relatives, but you might prefer that they check with you before coming to visit. You might want to read your book, but you might want to chat with your co-workers and give the impression of being friendly.

Saying It Straight

Training professional Abe Wagner is fond of saying, "Say it straight or you'll show it crooked!" His observation is accurate. Knowing what you want is not enough to be effective with other people. For a situation to turn out the way you want when others are involved, you also must know how to communicate directly and clearly.

CLEAR OR VAGUE?

Which of the following are straight communications that clearly convey what is wanted? Which are vague and unclear? Beside each communication, write the letter **C** for *clear* or **V** for *vague*.

1. ____ You wouldn't want to go to the movies tonight, would you?

2. ____ Why didn't you let us know you were coming?

3. ____ Will you please proofread this sometime today?

4. ____ You know, maybe we should postpone this until later.

5. ____ Please schedule a meeting with Fred and Mary to discuss the budget sometime next week.

6. ____ Are you sure you want to go camping this weekend?

7. ____ I would prefer to have more information about these new locations before making a commitment on the proposal.

8. ____ I want to be considered as a candidate for the position in Finance. Do I need to complete an application?

9. ____ Do you think you might be able to approve a raise for me in the next budget?

10. ____ I don't enjoy violence in movies. Will you suggest another movie or consider playing miniature golf instead?

Compare your answers with the authors' responses in the Appendix.

Communicating Clearly

You may have seen some patterns emerge in the communications in the exercises above. Using I-statements and well-worded directives and requests will help you be clear and straightforward.

I-Statements

Rather than expect the other person to read your mind from a vaguely worded or indirect request, simply state what you want beginning your sentence with "I…" as in these examples:

> *"I want to visit the tropical rain forest someday."*

> *"I feel like doing something fun tonight."*

> *"I would appreciate your asking me before telling other people that I will participate."*

Practice writing I-statements to communicate your wants in the following situations.

Relatives arrive for an unannounced visit.

_____

_____

Your boss gives you a complex assignment with only 24 hours to complete it.

_____

_____

Directives and Requests

When you need the cooperation of others to get what you want, be clear and straightforward, as in the question "Will you please?" Other requests—do you think you might, can you, could you, why don't you—are more tentative and passive and less likely to get cooperation. Here are examples of a clear directive and a straightforward request:

"Please read this and tell me what you think about it."

"Will you please approve a raise for me in the next budget?"

Practice being clear and straightforward in the following examples:

Write a directive (command) that instructs someone to prepare a report for you.

_____

_____

Write a request asking someone to do something with you.

_____

_____

CASE STUDY: Seeking Cooperation

Marti is frustrated because the sales representatives in her region do not consistently get their biweekly reports to her on time. She is talking about this with Tom, a fellow office employee: "I don't know how I am going to get those sales reps to cooperate! I have told them again and again that they need to have their reports to me by the deadline, and half of them just ignore me!" Tom asks, "Is it always the same ones who are late?" Marti answers, "A couple of them are almost always late, but each report period some of the others miss the deadline too. I never know which ones it will be, but I don't think I have ever had all of them on time."

Does Marti have a clear understanding with all of the sales representatives about their reports?

❏ Yes   ❏ No

Has Marti asked for a clear commitment?

❏ Yes   ❏ No

What do you recommend that Marti do to improve the situation?

_____

_____

_____

_____

_____

_____

_____

_____

Compare your answers to the authors' comments in the Appendix.

Negotiating Contractual Agreements

Most of what we accomplish requires the cooperation and support of other people. Clear communication helps to get this cooperation but does not guarantee it. To improve your chances of getting willing cooperation and commitment from others, use a contractual approach. This requires a two-way communication or negotiation that results in a clear understanding of who will do what and when.

Contract Guidelines

To better understand the contractual approach, consider what a contract is. It is an agreement between two or more people in which each promises something to the other. To ensure the agreement will be honored, the contract should be structured to meet the basic requirements of a valid contract.

1. **Each party clearly states wants/needs and each clearly agrees.**

   Each asks, "Will you please...?"
   Each responds, "Yes, I will."

2. **All parties benefit from the agreement.**

   If only one person gains, the others may feel victimized later and break their promise. When each person benefits, everyone has some motivation to keep the agreement.

3. **All parties can do what they promise.**

   All must have the ability and resources to do what they promise and accept the responsibility of being accountable for carrying out their commitment. This guideline is often broken when people make unrealistic time commitments.

4. **The agreement must be legal.**

   If the contract violates a law or established policy or rule, or if it conflicts with a previously negotiated agreement, it is an unenforceable contract. To avoid disappointment and conflict, make sure that agreements stay within the rules.

Practice Establishing Agreements

Bill is in charge of a project to develop new product concepts and marketing projections. He and his team have decided that to do a good job, they need more time and funding. They need to use a consulting firm for marketing research, and they need time to evaluate consultant proposals. Bill is planning to approach his boss, Joan, to negotiate for the time and money. Help Bill prepare by completing the following:

What can Bill offer to Joan as a benefit for her?

_____

_____

Write an I-statement and a request for Bill to use when asking Joan for what he wants.

_____

_____

Jennifer and Lisa work in a retail business. They are good friends. Lisa has an opportunity to attend a social hour with a new friend and to go with him to a concert after dinner. She is excited about the evening and hopes to convince Jennifer to close out her cash register and prepare her daily report so she can leave right at closing time to prepare for this special date. Help Lisa with her negotiating by completing the following:

What can Lisa offer Jennifer as a benefit?

_____

_____

Write an I-statement and a request for Lisa to use.

_____

_____

Compare your answers with the authors' responses in the Appendix.

Recognizing Conflict Roles

When people do not have clear and fair agreements, conflict often results. Preventing such situations is a major reward of using the win-win philosophy and the open, honest negotiation of the contractual approach. Not all conflict can be prevented, however, and resolving conflict can be one of the most difficult tests for the self-empowered person.

A valuable explanation of how conflict happens was developed by psychologist Stephen Karpman.* He recognized that conflict involves people playing predictable roles with one another, and he arranges these roles in a triangle.

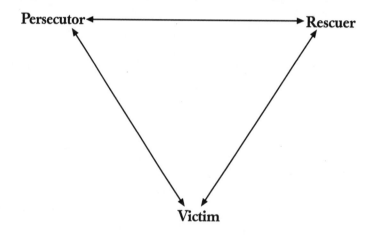

Let's take a look at the interaction among each of these roles in the following situations.

Conflict in the Doctor's Office

Carl has been waiting about 30 minutes in the reception area to see his doctor when a nurse calls in another patient who arrived after him. Carl charges to the receptionist's desk and bellows, "What's going on here? I've been wasting my time out here for half an hour, and now you're letting someone in to see the doctor before me! I demand that you get me in there right now!"

---

*Stephen Karpman, "Fairy Tales and Script Drama Analysis," *Transactional Analysis Bulletin VII, No. 26.*

The receptionist replies, "Oh, I'm so sorry. I don't know how this has happened, but I can't leave the desk unattended, and I'm sure the doctor will see you soon if you'll just wait a little longer." Carl roars, "If I don't get to see the doctor right now, I'm going to get a new doctor and I'll make sure your boss knows you were the cause!"

The office manager, Rachel, walks up and says, "Carl, I apologize for this mix-up, and I will instruct the nurse to take you right into exam room B and let the doctor know that you have been waiting quite some time. I'm sure he will get to you as soon as possible."

Who is playing the role of Persecutor? _____

Who is playing the role of Victim? _____

Who is playing the role of Rescuer? _____

Conflict in the Copy Center

Beverly has just received 85 copies of the handout material she will use for a presentation to all of her company's regional and district managers and top executives. She discovers that two pages are missing entirely and that other pages contain several errors. She is dismayed to see that none of the illustrations were printed in color as she requested. She runs to the copy center.

"You idiots have ruined my presentation! I know I can't expect much from this joke of a department, but this is the worst screw-up yet and I'm going to make sure the president hears about this one!" Jack, the copy center manager, responds, "What right do you have to come down here yelling at us? You always bring your stuff in at the last minute and expect us to work miracles for you! If you want perfect work, you'd better get your act together and allow some realistic lead time, lady!"

Who is playing the role of Persecutor? _____

Who is playing the role of Victim? _____

Who is playing the role of Rescuer? _____

Conflict over a Difficult Assignment

Kelly is struggling with how to present some figures as part of an important report that is due soon. After hearing deep sighs of frustration and seeing Kelly wad up page after page and throw them into the wastebasket, Stacy walks over and says, "Why don't you show them that information in a pie chart? Being able to see all of those figures in a visual form should help make the relationships of the figures more obvious."

Kelly responds, "Why couldn't I think of that? I never can figure out anything that involves so many numbers."

Who is playing the role of Persecutor? _____

Who is playing the role of Victim? _____

Who is playing the role of Rescuer? _____

Identifying the Conflict Roles

Did you recognize which individuals in the situations above were playing which roles? Compare your answers with the authors' below:

➤ In the doctor's office, Carl is the Persecutor, the receptionist is the Victim, and the office manager, Rachel, is the rescuer.

➤ In the copy center, Beverly first feels like a Victim and then becomes a Persecutor. Jack probably feels like the Victim of Beverly's attack and retaliates by playing Persecutor. The role of Rescuer was not involved.

➤ In the difficult assignment, Kelly is acting like a Victim with repeated sighs and histrionics. Stacy plays the role of Rescuer. There was no Persecutor.

Interpreting Conflict Interaction

The situations and reactions outlined above are all too common. We must recognize our own roles in similar cases because all three roles are undesirable ways to deal with people. To understand the truth of this, let's examine these three situations to explain how each role has negative consequences.

The Doctor's Office

Carl's persecutory behavior communicates disrespect for the receptionist, which is an "I'm okay—you're not okay," win-lose approach. If he gets his way with this behavior, he is likely to use the same approach again and again, alienating people and setting himself up for retaliation. Self-empowered people get their wants and needs met with win-win approaches rather than intimidation.

What could Carl have said if he were self-empowered?

_____

_____

Rachel, the receptionist, behaved as a Victim by cowering under Carl's attack and acting helpless about what to do. Self-empowered people do not allow others' behavior to get in the way of thinking clearly and feeling okay about themselves.

What could the receptionist have said to demonstrate self-empowerment?

_____

_____

Rachel's role is the most subtly inappropriate because the role of Rescuer appears desirable at first glance. But when one person steps in uninvited to rescue another, that action communicates a lack of respect for the Victim. Rescuing people reinforces their helplessness rather than helping them to become self-empowered. Later the Rescuer (Rachel) might feel like a Victim herself because she did all the work. Then the Rescuer might move to Persecutor and tell the Victim (receptionist) how poor a job she did, and then…You get the idea: people can run around the Drama Triangle endlessly.

If Rachel were self-empowered, she would allow the receptionist to handle the situation and would become involved only upon request. She also would provide training for the receptionist to develop skills for dealing with irate customers, thus empowering her.

The Copy Center

Beverly took her Victim feelings and turned them into a Persecutor attack on Jack, which invites retaliation and continuing resentment. It also results in a loss of respect from everyone who hears about it.

What would a self-empowered Beverly have said?

_____

_____

Jack reacted just like Beverly, allowing her words to trigger bad feelings and a retaliatory attack. His response will further strain their working relationship and make it more difficult for them to resolve the situation in a win-win manner.

What would a self-empowered Jack have said?

_____

_____

The Difficult Assignment

Kelly feels helpless and sends out subtle Victim messages, hoping a Rescuer is in the vicinity. This is like announcing, "I'm not okay—you're okay," which is not a self-empowered win-win approach. Kelly may get help in this passive manner, but at the cost of others perceiving her as less capable than they are.

What would a self-empowered Kelly have said to get help?

_____

_____

Stacy steps in to rescue Kelly with a good suggestion but probably feels less respectful of Kelly, at least at a subconscious level, and may resent Kelly's not doing her own work. The rescue also reinforces Kelly's inferiority about numbers and does not help her learn to ask for assistance in a self-empowered manner. Stacy could have demonstrated self-empowerment by acknowledging Kelly's frustration and asking if Kelly would like some suggestions. Even more empowering for Kelly would be for Stacy to use probing questions to prompt Kelly to think of her own solutions.

Communicating to Avoid Conflict

The more consistently you interact with others in a self-empowered manner, the fewer conflicts you will help to create. You will never be able to control the words, actions, or feelings of others, nor will you completely stop playing Persecutor, Rescuer, and Victim. Everyone learns to play these roles early in life, and we never seem to give them up entirely. But reducing your own frequency of participation in conflict with others by even a small percentage will feel wonderful, and you will gain respect from others.

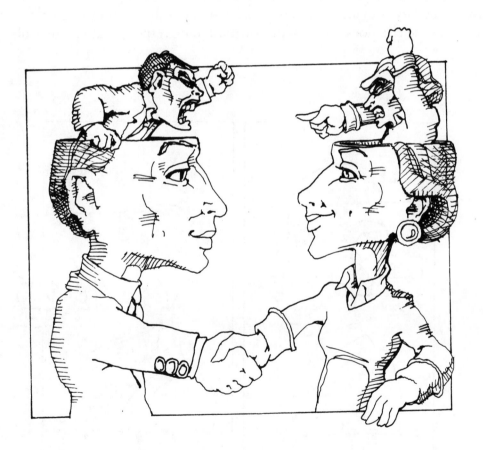

Improving Listening Skills

In many interactions with others the most important interpersonal skill is listening. No matter how skillfully one person chooses and delivers the words, communication does not occur if the other person does not listen. Self-empowered people know that good listening skills demonstrate respect for others and improve the odds for successful win-win interactions.

Ideally, a listener provides a response that proves to the speaker that he or she has been heard and understood. The ideal response also confirms for the listener that what was heard was understood accurately.

Most people go through their entire lives without receiving any instruction or training about how to listen. We all assume that because we have ears we know how to listen. Because we haven't been taught how to listen, however, most of us have learned by copying the listening behaviors of others, and we listen just the way everyone else does. Most of our own listening responses are predictable.

WHAT WOULD YOU SAY?

How would you respond if you were the listener in each of these examples?
Write your response in the space provided.

1. "I think I'll quit this crummy job! Management doesn't even know I
   exist, and only college graduates ever get promoted here."

   _____

   _____

2. "Mommy! Daddy! Billy said he doesn't like me anymore and he won't
   ever play with me again!"

   _____

   _____

3. "Look what you made me do! Why are you always sneaking around
   looking over my shoulder?"

   _____

   _____

4. "Why do we have to have all of these meetings? Most of them are a
   waste of time and boring to boot!"

   _____

   _____

5. "Please arrange a conference with the media department to discuss
   the new campaign. Be sure to check with the client about the deadline date and prepare a summary of the progress reports for everyone who will be in the meeting."

   _____

   _____

COMPARE YOUR RESPONSES

Most people respond in predictable ways to situations like those described in the listening exercise. Review the responses you wrote, and see how they compare with the following responses commonly given.

Situation 1:

Did you ask specific questions, offer advice, or say something encouraging? Fill in the blank with which type of response you chose or with a label that describes your response if it is different from these three.

_____

Situation 2:

Most parents say something reassuring or explain that Billy will change his mind after he has calmed down. Write which one you used, or label your response if it is different from these two.

_____

Situation 3:

Did you respond by apologizing, by attempting to explain your actions logically, or by saying something critical about the speaker's behavior? Write which response you used, or label your response if you used a different one.

_____

CONTINUED

Situation 4:

Some people respond by agreeing with the speaker, while others explain why the meetings are necessary, or they say something humorous, or they attempt to calm the speaker with reassurances. Write which of these you used, or label your response if it is different.

_____

Situation 5:

Most people say "Okay" or "Yes, sir" or "Yes, ma'am"–agreeing or complying. Some might ask a question, and a few might even make a sarcastic remark such as "Yes, your Royal Highness!" Write which response you used, or a label for your response if it was different.

_____

Any of your listening responses that were different from the most likely ones noted will be examined later. For now let's consider how the most common responses often fall short of ideal and how they might create communication problems.

Evaluating Common Responses

Some of our habitual listening responses do not confirm that we have heard correctly and do not provide any proof for ourselves that our understanding is correct. Such responses will not necessarily produce an adverse effect. But any time you use one of these responses, you take a risk of creating a communication roadblock or even conflict. To illustrate, consider the common responses explained below.

Questioning

When the listener starts asking specific questions, the speaker will usually answer, which often results in the listener unintentionally directing the communication away from what the speaker wanted to share or think about. A common form of question is the *closed question,* which can be answered yes or no. These questions tend to shut down communication.

Advice

One undesirable outcome of offering advice can occur when the person acts on the advice and it proves to be bad advice—the person will return to Persecute. Or if the advice proves to be good, the person will be back for more, which also can be undesirable! Another pitfall of giving advice is that the speaker may reject every offered suggestion (Yes, but...), which results in both people feeling frustrated.

Sympathy or Reassurance

A pitfall of this well-intended response is that the speaker may interpret it as insincere or patronizing. Even if it is accepted as genuine, another risk is that the person will become dependent upon this support and will continue to seek it by playing a Victim looking for a Rescuer.

Logical Explanation

This response is used frequently when the speaker has said something critical of the listener. But rational explanations usually accomplish little because the speaker is operating in an emotional or judgmental mode and hears the rationale as making excuses.

Apology

Apologizing is almost an automatic response when someone accuses the listener. But it can sound like Victim, which only encourages the person in the role of Persecutor to continue the attack. An apology is called for when you have behaved inappropriately.

Retaliation

Saying something critical or sarcastic to the speaker is another common reaction when the listener feels attacked or taken advantage of. All it will accomplish is to fan the flame of conflict.

Humor

Humor can be a valuable way to defuse an emotional situation, but frequently the listener's attempt at humor will be heard as criticism or as an indication that the listener does not take the situation seriously. This can lead to conflict.

Agreement

If the listener agrees with the speaker's opinions or position, the speaker may decide to do something foolish because he heard that he is "right." Later he will blame the listener for encouraging him. In situation 5, if the listener agrees to the directions by saying "Okay," the risk is that part of the instructions were misunderstood and an unnecessary mistake could occur.

A New Approach

This may be valuable. We are not telling you that these popular listening responses are always wrong. There is often no adverse effect when you respond in these ways. However, any time you use one of these responses you take a risk that you will end up in a conflict situation that could have been avoided if you had used a different listening approach. We will explain how to respond differently before concluding this section.

Avoiding Possible Pitfalls

If, on the exercise on page 47, you used any listening responses other than the ones we predicted on pages 48–49, please write a label for each of your responses in the spaces below. Next, think about how each of these responses might in any way result in undesirable outcomes. You may want to ask another person to contribute their ideas about the possible pitfalls associated with your responses.

Your response:

_____

Possible pitfalls:

_____

_____

_____

Your response:

_____

Possible pitfalls:

_____

_____

_____

Your response:

_____

Possible pitfalls:

_____

_____

_____

Listening to Foster Communication

Some listening responses are much more effective in communicating attentiveness and understanding, and thus less likely to add to or create conflict. You probably already use some of these. Becoming more aware of your responses is a step toward self-empowerment.

Attentiveness Signals

You demonstrate attentiveness by making good eye contact, nodding occasionally, looking interested with facial expressions and body postures. The occasional "Uh-huh," "I see," "I hear you," and so on also communicate attentiveness. These signals create the impression you are listening, but they prove nothing about whether you have understood a single word.

Prompting Signals

To encourage the speaker to open up or elaborate, you can say: "Tell me more," "Please continue," "Go on," or ask: "Then what happened?" "What more would you like me to know?" or "What are your thoughts on that?" These are *open* directives or questions that allow the speaker to say whatever she wants to communicate. They do not have the pitfalls of the closed or specific question. But these signals do not prove that you have heard anything correctly.

Oral Restatement

To prove that you heard and understood correctly, restate what you think the speaker just said to you. This is often called *active listening*. Use the following three-part formula for a restatement that will convey both your empathy and understanding.

1. **Paraphrase content**

    Abbreviate or reword the information or thoughts communicated by the speaker. This will prove that you understood.

2. **Acknowledge feelings**

    Listen to the voice and interpret body language signals to detect what feelings the speaker may be experiencing–most people won't say–and orally acknowledge these feelings. This will prove that you have empathy.

3. **Ask a checkout question**

    End your restatement with a brief question such as "Right?" or "Did I hear you correctly?" This allows the speaker to respond to your feedback, and it keeps the communication flowing.

Examples:

Craig: *"Oh no! I forgot to submit my expenses yesterday! Now it will be another month before I get reimbursed!"*

Sally: *"Gosh, Craig, you sound worried about having to wait so long for your reimbursement, right?"*

Craig: *"You bet I am! I need that money now!"*

Notice that Sally proved she had understood accurately, and she demonstrated empathy by acknowledging Craig's concern. Craig knows he has been heard by someone who cares, and Sally knows that she heard correctly. Sally also has avoided playing Rescuer.

Jim: *"Boy, Dan, you've really put me in a bind. I needed that information today to complete my report. My boss is going to kill me!"*

Dan: *"You seem disappointed that I don't have the information for you, Jim. Is that right?"*

Jim: *"No, Dan, I'm angry! You've got me in real trouble."*

Notice that Dan was inaccurate about Jim's feelings, and Jim immediately corrected him. Dan was correct with the content feedback, and the communication continued. Now Dan can acknowledge Jim's anger and concern about being in trouble, which will help them resolve this with a win-win outcome.

Perfecting Active Listening

➤ Avoid using the same opening phrase with your feedback. After the third "I hear you saying..." your responses will sound insincere or mechanical.

➤ Watch out for exaggerating or minimizing the other person's emotional level.

➤ Concentrate on what the person is actually saying and do not attempt to guess about what he is not saying. You don't want to come across as a psychoanalyst!

➤ If the other person notices that you are restating and responds defensively, simply explain that you are only attempting to make sure that you are understanding correctly. Most people will accept your restating when they understand its purpose.

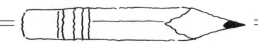

PRACTICE ACTIVE LISTENING

Write the missing portions of the verbal restatements for the examples below.

1. "Here comes Mrs. Green! She always complains about our music and about not having enough selections in her size!"

   "You seem _____ about having to deal with Mrs.

   Green's _____, right?"

2. "Dadgum it! I've added this three times and I get a different answer every time!"

   "Sounds like you're _____ with _____.

   Am I on target?

3. "You never think of anyone but yourself! Why don't you ever ask what I would like to do?"

   "I hear that you think _____ and you sound pretty

   _____. Is that right?"

Compare your answers with the authors' responses in the Appendix.

Resolving Conflict Through Active Listening

Active listening helps resolve conflicts. When you are faced with someone play-ing any one of the three conflict roles—Victim, Persecutor, or Rescuer—use the three-part feedback formula. This lowers the emotional level while preventing you from stepping into one of the conflict roles. When people feel empathy and understanding, they more quickly step out of a conflict role and communicate in a more reasonable and rational manner.

Your self-empowered skill of active listening helps keep you out of conflict and helps other people join you in win-win negotiation. Everyone benefits—which is the whole idea of being self-empowered and using the win-win philosophy.

In this section you have learned how you can improve your interpersonal skills to develop self-empowerment. Self-empowered people are effective not only in getting what they want, but also in doing so in a manner that empowers others by communicating respect and facilitating win-win outcomes.

In the next section you will learn how to improve management skills, allowing you to be more self-empowered in supervising others. Such skills are equally valuable in personal relationships.

Management Skills

60

Interacting with Your Employees

The most challenging aspect of management is dealing constantly with the most complicated creatures on earth—human beings. In the previous section you learned how to deal with people because you must be self-empowered to be in a management or supervisory position. It is much easier for the self-empowered person to handle management responsibilities and the stress that accompanies people management. Without self-empowerment, the manager's role can be a constant stream of anxiety-producing moments.

The skills in which managers are most frequently weak have a common characteristic: they require face-to-face interaction with employees. Many managers are good at planning, making decisions, solving problems, and using time efficiently, but few are truly skillful at interacting with the people they manage.

This section focuses on improving your people skills in specific management situations that often prove difficult. By developing more skill in supervisory functions, you will be building your self-confidence and competency, which will add to your growing self-empowerment. Only the self-empowered manager is good at empowering others. When you become a skilled manager, everyone will benefit—you, your employees, and your organization.

Even if you are not a supervisor, team leader, or manager, you will benefit from learning the techniques and skills in this part. You will gain a better understanding of what your manager does, and you will be better qualified to move into a management role yourself. You also will discover that some of these ideas relate to dealing with people in other contexts, such as home, volunteer organizations, church, community involvement, and social interactions.

EVALUATE YOUR MANAGEMENT SKILLS

Rate yourself between 1 and 5 on each of the management skills listed below.

1 = weak   3 = acceptable   5 = excellent

1. Setting goals and priorities	1	2	3	4	5
2. Keeping employees informed	1	2	3	4	5
3. Delegating responsibility to employees	1	2	3	4	5
4. Solving problems and making decisions	1	2	3	4	5
5. Coaching employees when they make mistakes	1	2	3	4	5
6. Giving positive recognition	1	2	3	4	5
7. Seeking input and ideas from employees	1	2	3	4	5
8. Confronting problem behavior	1	2	3	4	5
9. Giving meaningful performance evaluations	1	2	3	4	5
10. Using your time efficiently	1	2	3	4	5

How did you do? Did you recognize some management skills that could use improvement? Few managers are excellent in all of the skills listed above, so if you rated yourself less than 4 or 5 on some, you have a lot of company.

If you have the courage, ask each employee to rate you on these same skills to find out how they perceive you as a manager. You might learn that you are not as good at some of these as you think you are.

CASE STUDY: Delegating or Dumping?

Marvin asks Tony and Ellen to join him in his office. He says to Tony, "The monthly production figures are too hard to use, and it's taking too much of my time to analyze all this stuff. Take this report and summarize each section for me. Also break out the comparison figures for the improvement over last year for each team. I'll want you to do this for me each month, Tony, okay?" Tony responds, "Uh, sure. I'll get right on it."

Marvin turns to Ellen and says, "Ellen, I've been getting lots of complaints from the shop supervisors that the support staff are uncooperative. They're going to have to understand that their job is to provide assistance to everyone in this organization and that includes the shop supervisors. I need you to get that across to them." He looks expectantly at Ellen who answers, "I'll talk to them in the staff meeting Monday, but I know they are going to complain that the shop supervisors don't give them enough time to..." Marvin interrupts Ellen and says, "I don't want the hear their excuses. I want you to make sure they start doing a better job! That's all. You both can get back to work now."

How do you rate Marvin's delegation skills? Check (✔) each item below that you think he needs to improve and compare your answers with the authors'.

___ Instructions are specific and clear.

___ The employee is given enough authority to do the job.

___ The manager confirms that the employee understood accurately.

___ The employee is given authority to make decisions and suggestions.

___ Responsibility for results rather than a specific task is delegated.

___ The employee receives encouragement and positive expectations.

___ A system for follow-up evaluation is established.

___ The employee is encouraged to ask clarifying questions.

Compare your answers to the authors' comments in the Appendix.

Delegating to Empower Others

As you have seen in the previous case study, being an effective manager means knowing when and how to delegate. Skillful delegation empowers employees to accept responsibility for how they carry out the delegation. But for many reasons, managers of all levels fail to delegate skillfully.

Why Is Delegating So Difficult?

List as many reasons as you can to explain why people find delegation difficult to do well.

_____

_____

_____

_____

_____

_____

When managers are asked to identify the reasons they don't delegate, these are the most common answers:

➤ **I don't trust my employees.** Too many people still believe the old saying "If you want something done right, do it yourself."

➤ **It takes longer to delegate than to do it myself.** This is often a rationalization because the actual time difference may be negligible. Even when the statement is true, the manager will probably have to do this same task again and again. Investing a little time today saves a lot of time in the future.

➤ **I enjoy doing it myself.** This is a common reason for holding on to jobs that could be delegated. Good managers know that they must look beyond their own preferences and consider what is best for accomplishing goals, for the entire organization, for the development of employees, and so on.

➤ **I don't have anyone with experience or skills.** This is a good reason for being reluctant to delegate, but the solution is obvious: provide training.

➤ **I'm afraid they might do it better than I can.** This is scary if you are not self-empowered. Smart managers understand that you can't be the best at everything. You will impress people more by knowing how to use the strengths of your team than by trying to do everything yourself.

Preparing to Delegate

A self-empowered manager knows that delegation is a complex skill that requires preparation and good communication skills. To help you improve your delegation skills, answer the following questions before each delegation:

1   What is the goal or objective of delegating this task or responsibility?

Answering this question identifies the delegation's expected outcome. This will help you to delegate a responsibility for outcome rather than just a meaningless task.

Example: Marvin could have defined his delegation goal as redesigning the production reports to produce information that could be used without so much additional analysis.

Practice: Define the delegation goal for the problem that was given to Ellen in the earlier example.

_____

_____

2 Whom will I select for this assignment?

This question requires you to consider your candidates. Who is the most qualified? Who would most like to do this? Who needs the growth experience? Who has the time? Who could handle this with some training?

Example: Marvin might have selected Tony because he is familiar with production, likes working with numbers, and has a good relationship with the production team.

Practice: What factors might Marvin have considered in choosing Ellen for the other delegation?

_____

_____

3 What kind of authority or power is needed and how much is required?

This answer is important if the person is to be empowered enough to be successful. Assigning a responsibility without giving appropriate power will almost always guarantee failure.

Example: Marvin would need to give Tony authority to ask the production people for different data, to experiment with different formats, and possibly to call upon people in other departments such as accounting, quality assurance, and data processing for assistance.

Practice: What authority would Ellen need for her assignment?

_____

_____

4 Who else needs to know about this delegation?

Your employee has authority only when others know that you have given this power. Think about all who may be involved in carrying out this delegation and inform each one about it.

Example: To assure Tony's success, Marvin would need to inform the production crew, accounting, quality assurance, and data processing that Tony has authority to request their help with the project.

Practice: Who would need to know about Ellen's assignment and the extent of her authority?

---

5 What type of control or feedback will I need?

A major concern about delegating is the loss of control, so you need to figure out how you can reduce this stress factor. What kind of information will you want about progress and how often? How will you meet your need for control so you avoid looking over your employee's shoulder (which communicates distrust)?

Example: Marvin might want Tony to discuss new format designs with him before implementing them. He might want a weekly progress report.

Practice: What controls or feedback would Marvin want in Ellen's case?

---

6 What is a reasonable time limit for completion?

You may want to involve the employee in answering this question. A clear deadline helps to focus efforts and increases the probability of success. The time limit needs to be realistic for both your needs and your employee's.

Example: For Tony's assignment, a reasonable time limit might be several months or longer to allow for experimentation with different reporting formats and for developing the computer programming. It could take longer, depending on the amount of data needed and the complexity of the redesign challenge.

Practice: What would be a reasonable time limit for Ellen's assignment of resolving the conflict between the shop supervisors and the support staff?

_____

_____

7 When and how will we evaluate the performance?

Planning for evaluation ensures you will identify the measures of success and arrange a system for providing the information needed for evaluation. The employee deserves positive reinforcement of a good performance and coaching assistance with any problems.

Example: Marvin and Tony will need to evaluate how well the new reporting system provides the needed data. They also will want to evaluate how Tony went about resolving the problem. The evaluation might include asking others who were involved to evaluate Tony's role.

Practice: What aspects of Ellen's performance will need to be evaluated and how might this be done?

_____

_____

Planning for delegation is essential to ensure the assignment will be completed successfully. Delegation is an important opportunity to strengthen your relationship with employees and to empower them so that everyone benefits.

THE DELEGATION DISCUSSION

The next major step in delegating is communicating with the person selected for the assignment. Use the following guidelines to assist you with this important communication challenge:

> **Meet face-to-face without time pressure.** Memos and e-mail messages are more likely to be misunderstood than oral give and take. Allow time for questions and to discuss alternatives. Summarize the agreements in writing after the meeting.

> **Ask rather than command.** Most people prefer to be asked rather than told what to do. It is a subtle demonstration of respect. Asking also requires a response from the employee while a command does not.

> **Check for understanding and commitment.** Don't ask "Do you understand?" or "Okay?" because most people will say yes even when they don't clearly understand. Ask the employee to summarize what you have discussed. You must receive a definite commitment; don't accept "I'll try" because this answer signals a potential failure.

> **Agree on the control procedures and the follow-up date.** If you and the employee agree about how you will be kept informed, you will not need to check up. If you both know in advance when and how the performance will be evaluated, the delegation is more likely to be successful.

> **Inform others about the delegation.** Your delegation is not complete until you have told everyone who may be affected or involved.

CASE STUDY: Delegating to Empower

Marvin asks Tony to join him in his office. "Tony, I'm having trouble using the production figures. I have to spend too much time analyzing the data. I know that you are familiar with production and that you are good with numbers. You also have a solid relationship with the production people, so I would like for you to figure out a better way to report this information. Are you willing to take this on?"

Tony responds, "I would love to! What are the biggest problems with the way the information is reported now?"

Marvin answers, "I can't tell at a glance how each team is doing on production goals or in comparison to the other teams. I also have to spend a lot of time looking up last year's performance figures to check our improvement."

Tony says, "Okay, that gives me a better idea of what you need. May I get some help from Sherry in data processing? She is our best programmer, and I'll bet she'll have some good ideas about how to get this data reported in more useful ways."

Marvin answers, "Sure, Tony, and I'll authorize whatever computer time you two will need. I'll also tell all of the production people that you are going to need their cooperation. Anything else?" Tony says, "Not right now, but I may have more questions later." Marvin ends with, "Ask anytime, Tony. Will you give me a weekly progress report and present your ideas to me before we make any changes in the system?" "Sure, boss."

See the authors' comments to this case study in the Appendix.

Do Your Own Delegation

Write your ideas about how to delegate the other assignment to Ellen.
Practice with a friend or family member.

_____

_____

_____

_____

_____

_____

_____

_____

_____

_____

_____

_____

_____

_____

_____

Receiving a Delegated Assignment

You might be thinking to yourself, "Okay, fine. Now I know how to delegate, but my boss sure doesn't! How does this help me when I'm on the receiving end of a delegation?"

Good question. Self-empowered employees take the initiative to help themselves receive an effective delegation so they can be sure to carry out the assignment as well as possible. Consider these strategies:

➤ If the boss is being vague with the assignment or is giving you a task rather than responsibility for a result, you can ask a question such as "To help me understand my assignment, what is the outcome you want me to achieve?" When the boss answers this question, a better delegation may result.

➤ If your boss fails to explain how much power or what kind of authority you have for carrying out the assignment, probe the issue along these lines: "It seems to me that if I am going to be responsible for improving the delivery time, I will need the authority to ask the salespeople and the order fulfillment and shipping departments to help me make some changes. Will you please tell them that I have your authorization?"

Do you get the idea? If your boss does not delegate skillfully, you can help by asking questions. Your boss most likely will be impressed by your initiative and will appreciate having a better-defined agreement with you. By doing this you can be more comfortable with the delegated responsibility and the ultimate accountability for the results you are expected to achieve.

Recovering and Learning from Mistakes

One of the challenges in fostering self-empowerment is responding to the employee who makes a mistake. Managers in organizations of all types and sizes too often respond to mistakes in a disapproving or punitive manner. Such a response has a detrimental effect on self-empowerment.

The Cost of Mishandling Mistakes

When mistakes result in angry lectures, suspension or probation, reductions in income, written documentation of poor performance, or even termination of employment—all common responses—an unwritten rule is being communicated to employees: that employees should never make mistakes. Is this realistic? Of course not, but this perception exists in most organizations and work groups. When this is the unwritten expectation, how do employees approach their work?

If you said cautiously or fearfully, you realize the problem of treating mistakes harshly. Yet time and time again, employees receive only punitive responses. No wonder so many resist change and efforts to improve. They know that changing things increases the probability of making mistakes, and they are not going to take that chance if they don't have to. Why set oneself up for punishment?

Possibly the biggest price organizations pay for treating mistakes punitively is the lesson employees learn about making a mistake. What do people learn to do about a mistake they have made?

Everyone knows the answer is cover it up. Why do managers continue to handle mistakes so badly when the cost to themselves and the organization is so obvious? The simple answer is that no one has taught them how to do it better. All of our lives we have been criticized by parents, teachers, and our own bosses for making mistakes. How were we supposed to learn a positive, helpful way to treat others' mistakes?

CASE STUDY: One Mistake Leads to Another

Tony and Sherry have responded enthusiastically to their challenge and have generated many ideas about how to improve the production reporting. They have designed a new form for the supervisors to use in reporting the information to data processing, so they will have what they need for a newly designed report to Marvin.

Predictably, the supervisors are resistant to changing, and they have complained to the production manager. The production manager tells Marvin, "Tony has my supervisors in an uproar, Marvin. They are complaining to me about all these new forms, and they don't understand why we're always changing things!"

Marvin encounters Tony in the hallway talking with Sherry and two other employees and says angrily, "Tony, I told you not to change any forms until you had cleared your ideas with me! You've got everyone in production mad. Not only have you not helped me with my problem—you've created a bigger one!"

A familiar scene? Tony has made a mistake, but Marvin has made an even bigger one, hasn't he? What are Marvin's mistakes?

_____

_____

_____

_____

Compare your answers to the authors' comments in the Appendix.

REACTING TO MISTAKES

Recall some of your own mistakes, and check (✔) each of the experiences below that were unpleasant for you.

❏   Feelings of self-disgust

❏   Anger about wasted time

❏   Fear of discovery

❏   Embarrassment

❏   Rebuke by boss, parent, or other

❏   Teasing by friends, peers

❏   Public reprimand

❏   Being asked for an explanation

❏   Lack of coaching help

❏   Punishment

You may have checked several choices because different mistakes produce different outcomes, and each person reacts differently to each response. Now reconsider those you checked and decide which one or two you dislike most and circle those. Do you think others might react similarly?

Coaching Employees Through Their Mistakes

Making mistakes is inevitable. But how you handle your employees' mistakes will make a difference in how they accept responsibility in the future. The self-empowered manager knows that mistakes are opportunities for coaching employees to:

➤ **Identify the cause of the mistake.**

➤ **Determine corrective actions.**

➤ **Learn how to prevent the recurrence of the same mistake.**

➤ **Be more comfortable being accountable.**

Coaching employees through their mistakes is a step-by-step process that helps them learn from their mistakes and helps managers improve working relationships. The sequence on the next page represents the self-empowered approach to handling others' mistakes.

1 Demonstrate respect, care, and reassurance.

The employee already feels bad about making a mistake. Say or do nothing to communicate disapproval. Show you care with statements such as "Everybody makes mistakes," "Don't punish yourself," or "You just proved you're human."

2 Share one of your own mistakes.

Tell the employee about one of your own mistakes to help him feel better and to build trust in your relationship. People are less likely to hide mistakes when they know you have made them too.

3 Ask one question and listen.

Ask an open-ended question such as "What happened?" or "How did this happen?" Keep quiet and allow time for the other to answer. If the employee is to learn from this mistake, she must do most of the thinking. By telling you how the mistake occurred, she will be more likely to remember what was done incorrectly. Do not ask a series of fact-finding questions because then you are doing all of the thinking.

4 Ask another question and listen.

When the employee has identified what was done incorrectly, ask, "How can you fix it?" Again, allow the other person to do the thinking. When employees think of solutions, they are much more likely to remember them and follow through than if you thought of a solution for them. If they don't know how, work together to identify possibilities.

5 Ask a final question and listen.

To help ensure the same mistake will not be repeated, ask, "How can you make sure this won't happen again?" Allow time for an answer, listen, and restate. When employees themselves figure out the actions needed to prevent recurrence, they are more likely to learn from the experience.

CASE STUDY: A Positive Learning Experience

Marvin learns from the production manager that Tony has designed new forms for the supervisors to report production results and that they are unhappy about all of the changes. He finds Tony in the hallway talking with Sherry and two other co-workers. He says, "Tony, when you finish here, will you check with me in my office?"

"Sure, Marvin. We just finished and I want to tell you about what Sherry and I have done anyway."

When Tony and Marvin return to Marvin's office, Marvin says, "Before you tell me about your project, let me share something with you. Franklin was just in here telling me about your new forms and how the supervisors are resisting the changes. I'm unhappy about this because I thought we agreed you would clear any new forms with me before implementing them. Was that our agreement?"

"Uh, yeah, I guess I got excited about our ideas and forgot to check it out with you. I'm sorry."

"That's okay, Tony. We all make mistakes. I remember that my first week on the job here I got so excited about the project I was working on that I did some work that was only supposed to be done by someone with security clearance. I had the security team all over me!"

"You're kidding!"

"Nope. I really did. So you're telling me that in your excitement you just forgot to clear your ideas with me and I can understand that. How can you get the supervisors to calm down and work with you on this?"

"I think it would be a good idea for me to tell them that I jumped the gun a little and apologize for not communicating with you and them about our ideas before presenting them with a new form."

Marvin responds, "That might do it, Tony. I'll help you out by meeting with all of you to provide moral support. About all I will say is that you are helping me to figure out ways to make our reporting more useful." (Pause) "How can you make sure something like this won't happen again?" Tony answers, "I think it would be a good idea for me to meet with you each week to discuss our progress rather than submitting a written report like I was doing."

Marvin says, "Good idea. Let's do it."

See the authors' comments to this case study in the Appendix.

Redefining People Problems

Dealing with people problems is possibly the greatest management challenge, requiring the highest degree of self-empowerment. This section presents problem-solving ideas to help you build self-empowerment.

Analyzing the Problem

Think of a circumstance in which someone has caused problems for you. Choose one that has been frustrating or difficult for you to resolve, then describe the problem you have had with the person.

_____

_____

_____

_____

_____

Now look back at your description and answer the following questions.

➤ Did you describe the problem by referring to the person with negative adjectives, or labels, such as lazy, uninterested, arrogant, or stupid?
_____

➤ Did you describe the problem by referring to the person's personality characteristics, attitudes, or motivational level, such as "has a bad attitude," "doesn't care," "has an insulting manner," or "does as little as she can get away with"? _____

➤ When you think about the problem, do you find yourself thinking that the person is the problem? _____

Most people find themselves answering "yes" to the above questions because most people have learned to define a problem as the other person—the person is the problem. That's why such problems have come to be called *people problems.*

Motivating People to Change

The most commonly heard complaints from managers are that employees have a "bad attitude" or are "just not motivated." When problems with others are defined in these ways, a successful win-win resolution is highly unlikely. Why? Because from all the research into personality, attitudes, and motivation over many decades, we know the following generally to be true:

➤ Personality is developed during the early years of childhood, and most experts in psychology and psychiatry agree that personality does not change once it is formed. Even with extensive psychotherapy, people do not change their basic personalities. These core characteristics are like the foundation of a house, which can be built upon through life—adding rooms or remodeling—but the foundation remains untouched.

➤ Attitudes reflect our core beliefs and values. Attitudes can change when a person's underlying beliefs and values change, but this generally happens only when the person decides to change, not when someone else attempts to change them. Change is most often prompted by a traumatic life event such as divorce, a major illness or accident, the death of a loved one, or a job loss.

➤ Motivation is a process of attempting to satisfy unsatisfied needs. A satisfied need does not produce motivated behavior. Offering a banana split to motivate you will be ineffective if you are feeling stuffed from eating a large meal. Some motivational needs are basic and predictable: the need to survive, to be safe from harm, to have enough to eat and drink. Other needs are unique to the individual and are much less predictable.

Changing someone else's motivational needs is generally not possible. About all anyone can do is to know individuals well enough to understand their motivational needs and then provide whatever will satisfy those needs in the hope of motivating them to act in desired ways.

So if we can't change someone's personality, attitudes, or motivational needs, how can we hope to resolve people problems? Fortunately, the answer is simple: Define the problem correctly. People problem is an unfortunate misnomer—the problem is not the person. The problem is the person's *behavior*. To help you learn this distinction, complete the following exercise.

IDENTIFY THE REAL PROBLEM

One of the greatest challenges with behavior problems is identifying the behavior rather than judging the person or assuming you know the reasons for the behavior. For each situation, write a label someone might use to describe the person and then describe the observable behavior more factually.

1. Sally remarks to Perry, "Where do you buy your clothes? I haven't seen an outfit like that since the circus was in town!"

   What label might describe Sally? _____

   What is her actual behavior? _____

   _____

2. For the fourth time this month, Jeremy's expense report is incomplete and contains several computational errors.

   What label could describe Jeremy? _____

   What is his actual behavior? _____

   _____

3. Will has just swatted Ann on her buttocks with a rolled-up magazine and said, "I sure like the way that skirt fits!"

   What label might be used to describe Will? _____

   What is his actual behavior? _____

   _____

4. Monica is shouting angrily at three of her employees, "Why can't you morons learn how to do this right? If you don't get your production figures up with the other team's, you're going to get yourselves fired!"

   What label might describe Monica? _____

   What is her actual behavior? _____

   _____

Compare your answers with the authors' responses in the Appendix.

Confronting Unacceptable Behavior

To resolve people's behavior problems, you must be willing to confront them about the behavior and negotiate with them to change. People can change behaviors much more easily than they can change their personality characteristics.

Fear of Confrontation

What is your reaction to the idea of confrontation? What do you imagine when you think about confronting someone? Check (✔) any of the responses below that fit your expectations about confrontation.

- ❏ The other person will get angry.

- ❏ I will feel nervous.

- ❏ The other person will make excuses.

- ❏ I will get angry.

- ❏ The other person will cry.

- ❏ The other person will resent me.

- ❏ The other person will dislike me.

- ❏ It will hurt the relationship.

- ❏ It won't accomplish anything.

- ❏ The other person will counterattack.

- ❏ The other person will think I'm petty.

- ❏ Everyone will gossip.

Most people have had only negative experiences with confrontation. Perhaps you were confronted by someone who did not handle the communication skillfully. Or you may have confronted someone else and had it turn out badly because you had no training in what to do. Both experiences would cause you to have negative expectations about confronting others.

Formulating a Positive Confrontation

It is possible for confrontation to be respectful and even caring. Confrontation can be appropriate and valuable for the person being confronted. After all, how can people improve and change behaviors that affect others negatively if no one will let them know they are doing something that is a problem?

The key to ensuring that confrontation produces positive outcomes is handling confrontation skillfully. A caring confrontation involves four steps:

1. Define the behavior.

2. Identify the impact upon you.

3. Identify your emotions.

4. Define your objective.

An exact formula cannot be devised for every situation. But when you are looking to produce a positive outcome and benefit all concerned, you should work through these four steps. With effort and practice, this caring approach to confrontation will become automatic.

1 Define the behavior.

Identify what the person does that you wish they did not do or what they do not do that you wish they would do. Define what they do that you wish they would do differently. Avoid using judgmental or accusatory words when you describe the behavior. Use a factual, nonblaming description to reduce defensive reactions.

Example: Arriving for work after 8:00 A.M., staying on break more than 15 minutes, telling customers they should have followed instructions.

Practice: Describe the behavior of the person in the problem situation you described on page 79. If you used labels before, describe the observed behavior that led you to attach that label.

----

2 Identify the impact upon you.

How does the other person's behavior create a measurable negative impact? What does it cost? Money? Time? Productivity? Perhaps several undesirable tangible effects could result from the behavior. Identify these possible results because you may want to explain one or more of them during your discussion.

Example: Others might match the behavior; others might feel angry or resentful, which would affect their productivity; the customer might buy elsewhere.

Practice: Think of your own problem situation and identify at least two or three ways the other person's behavior has had or could have an undesirable impact. List several possibilities to increase the likelihood that you will find one that will motivate the other person to change the behavior.

_____

_____

_____

3 Identify your emotions.

You are likely to respond emotionally when someone's behavior affects you negatively. If you do not express these feelings, they accumulate, which can result in your exploding inappropriately sometime later or at someone else who doesn't deserve your attack. If you store up too many unexpressed emotions, you can even create health problems. To help you identify the negative feelings involved, consider these basic emotion categories: mad, sad, and scared.

Example: Concerned that others will match the behavior, worried that others' resentment will affect productivity, and afraid that the customer will not return. You might also be disappointed or angry.

Practice: Identify your feelings in your own problem situation. You may want to note the feeling you have about each negative effect.

_____

_____

_____

4 Define your objective.

What do you hope to accomplish with your confrontation? Do you want the person to stop the behavior in question or to use a different behavior? Are you willing to have the person suggest alternatives? People are most likely to follow through and implement a change they thought of themselves.

Ask for what you want rather than using a command, which may sound intimidating and interfere with a successful negotiation outcome.

Example: "Will you please be at work by 8:00 A.M.?" "Will you please limit your breaks to 15 minutes?" What do you think would be a more effective approach to use with customers who complain about how the product works?

Practice: List one or more outcomes that would satisfy you in solving your own problem situation. You may want to consider several to increase the chances of a win-win compromise. Be sure to consider asking the other person for a suggested solution.

_____

_____

_____

Phrasing the Confrontation

Developing the four steps in the confrontation formula will help you prepare for discussion. Next comes planning what you will say. Write possible openings and other statements to make during the discussion. You may also rehearse until you can say the statements in a respectful, nonthreatening manner. Mental rehearsal helps to assure a successful negotiation. Remember to imagine positive pictures.

How might a confrontation sound? Consider the following examples for confronting the behaviors in the "Identify the Real Problem" exercise on page 81.

1. Perry could say to Sally, "Sally, I feel hurt and embarrassed when you make remarks about my clothes, particularly when you do it in front of others. Will you please not make such comments?"

2. You might say to Jeremy, "Jeremy, several of your expense reports have been incomplete and contained some errors. This results in my assistant taking time from other duties to contact you for the missing information and to correct your mistakes. I'm annoyed that his time is being used this way. Will you please be sure that your reports are complete and accurate?"

3. Ann could confront Will with, "Will, I strongly dislike your hitting me, and your remark about my skirt was inappropriate. Will you please apologize and never do that again?"

   Will's manager could confront Will because his behavior could harm the manager and the organization if Ann files a sexual harassment charge. The manager might say, "Will, I saw you swat Ann with your magazine and I heard you make a remark about her clothes. I'm disappointed you did that, and I'm concerned that Ann might charge sexual harassment if you do something like that again. Will you please make sure that your interaction with her is professional?"

4. Monica's employees could confront her by saying, "When you yell at us and threaten to fire us, we feel embarrassed and angry. We are concerned about maintaining a good relationship with you, and we're asking that you give us performance feedback in a more helpful manner."

Monica's manager would also have a reason to confront her because her behavior could affect productivity, turnover, and so on. The manager could say, "Monica, I'm concerned about how you handled that situation with your employees just now. Shouting and using threats might result in resentment and rebellion rather than improvement. What do you suggest as a better way to deal with those three?"

PREPARE YOUR OWN CONFRONTATION

It sounds easy when the words are provided, doesn't it? You can learn to confront appropriately and effectively, but it will require practice. Just preparing your answers to the four questions before the confrontation is not enough. Your skill will develop only with practice.

Complete your preparation for the problem situation you have used for practice, and have a discussion with the person soon. Only by having this discussion will you gain self-confidence and skill. When you do, you will have become significantly more self-empowered. You also help others realize they will be held accountable for their actions. Write below what you will say to the other person.

_____

_____

_____

Diffusing Emotional Reactions

After planning your confrontation, you might ask, "But what happens when I try this and the other person gets angry or starts crying or something like that?" You are right that a defensive response is a good possibility. People are not accustomed to being confronted appropriately, and they may react emotionally. When people become emotional they may cry, attack you angrily, deny their behavior, or make phony excuses.

What do you do when you hear someone being emotional?

_____

_____

_____

If you answered, "Restate their feelings and some content," congratulations! The best way to defuse defensive responses is to use your listening feedback skills. You might need to restate the other person's words and acknowledge his feelings a number of times before he calms down, but eventually he will. When he does, continue the discussion by saying something else.

You have the advantage of being prepared and effective when you have practiced both skills—confrontation and listening. What a sense of self-empowerment it is—and what a way to empower others—when you help negotiate a win-win agreement.

CASE STUDY: Confronting a Co-Worker

Kerry and Liu are teammates with very different personalities, but they have worked together successfully on several projects and have received commendations from their manager. Actually, in each project Liu was required to do some of the work that was supposed to be Kerry's responsibility. Liu has never complained about this.

While working on another project, Kerry has again failed to complete an analysis and the deadline is approaching. Liu decides this time to confront Kerry's behavior and get an agreement for change.

Help Liu prepare for this confrontation by completing the following items:

Describe Kerry's behavior using nonblaming words:

_____

_____

_____

What are some concrete and tangible effects that could result from this behavior?

_____

_____

_____

If you were in Liu's position, what emotions would you probably be feeling?

_____

_____

_____

What do suggest for Liu to ask of Kerry?

_____

_____

_____

Compare your answers to the authors' comments in the Appendix.

Plan What to Say

Using the elements you identified above or those provided by the authors, write the statements Liu might use to confront Kerry's recurring behavior.

_____

_____

_____

_____

_____

_____

Many word choices could be equally effective. Liu could say, "Kerry, I am disappointed that you have not completed your analysis. I am concerned that our project will not be done on time and we will receive a poor performance review from our manager. What do you suggest as a solution?"

Let's assume Liu delivers the words above in a calm, nonthreatening tone and Kerry replies, "I suggest you mind your own business!"

How do you recommend Liu respond to this angry retort?

_____

_____

_____

Respond with Active Listening

An active listening response would sound something like this: "Kerry, I hear that you are angry with me for bringing this up and that you think your not completing the analysis is none of my business. Right?"

Kerry might react: "You bet I'm angry! I work just as hard as you, and I resent your implying that I'm not doing my share of the work!"

How should Liu respond to this?

_____

_____

_____

Another active listening response: "You're telling me that you are upset with me because what I said sounded like an accusation to you. Is that true?"

Kerry responds again, "Well, you were saying that we might get a bad review from the boss because of me, weren't you?"

How might Liu respond to this last response from Kerry?

_____

_____

_____

How about a response along these lines: "Yes, Kerry, I did mention that a result of your analysis not being done on time might be an unfavorable evaluation of our work, which is why I wanted to talk with you and come up with a solution. What do you suggest we do to get back on track to finish our project on time?"

Summarizing the Confrontation

This series of interactions is typical of how a confrontation will evolve if the confronter knows how to handle the defensive responses. With a little empathy and understanding, Kerry became less defensive each time and allowed Liu to patiently return to the problem and a need for a solution.

Liu must not allow Kerry to get Liu to do the work. This would repeat the pattern they have been following, which results in Liu playing the role of Rescuer: Rescuing may solve the immediate problem, but it almost guarantees a continuation of the pattern of Kerry not doing the work and Liu picking up the slack.

Your Personal Development Program

Identifying Values and Priorities

You are on your way to becoming self-empowered now that you understand the principles of empowerment and the techniques for improving your interpersonal and management skills. Reading this book and completing the exercises will not transform you, but you can make significant changes by continuing to use what you have learned. Becoming self-empowered takes time and practice through a personal development plan.

This part will help you devise your own program because each person has different values and priorities. Being self-empowered means having more of what you want from life, so you have to identify what those "wants" are. The following exercise will help you clarify what to focus on in your personal development program.

WHAT IS IMPORTANT TO YOU?

As you learned in Part 4, what motivates one person to act may not motivate another. Knowing your own values and priorities is important to achieving your vision of success. Identify your values in each of the areas below.

1. **Work.** What is important to you about work? Do you value challenge, interesting work, recognition, involvement, power or control, self-expression or creativity, low stress? List all work-related elements important to you.

   _____

   _____

   _____

   _____

2. **Relationships.** Do you value having a loving family, many close friends, or a few, close relationships at work? Is it important for you to have relationships that involve love, trust, honesty, sexuality, sharing, companionship? List all your relationship values.

   _____

   _____

   _____

   _____

3. **Financial.** Do you value owning nice things, having extra money for travel, being financially secure and debt-free for your retirement years, or being wealthy with "money to burn"? List all your values related to finances.

   _____

   _____

   _____

   _____

CONTINUED

4. **Living.** Do you value health and physical fitness, recreation and play, arts, theater or other forms of entertainment, reading, learning, creativity, spirituality or religion, helping others, protecting the environment? List what you value about living in general.

_____

_____

_____

_____

5. **Other values.** What else is important to you? Do you want fame, to be remembered after you are gone, to contribute something that will benefit everyone, to see the world, to own your own business, to travel in space? What else? List all your other values.

_____

_____

_____

_____

Count the values you listed in all the categories. Divide the total by 3 and write the number here _____.

Establishing Priorities

One of the harsh realities of life is that you cannot have it all. You can enjoy great success and achieve most of your goals, but the likelihood of having all your values satisfied is small. To satisfy your most important values, you must establish priorities. Here are three priority categories and what each one means:

A = Highest priority

These values are most important to you. You may already have them in your life or you may be working to achieve them, but you value them very much.

B = Moderate priority

These values are important to you but less so than the A values. You would be more comfortable giving up one of these than one of the A values.

C = Lowest priority

These are the ones you value the least. You might like to have these in your life, but they are the values you are most willing to sacrifice to have your A and B values satisfied.

Write one of these priority letters beside each of the values you identified in the previous exercise, but put only one-third of the values into each category. The number of values in each category should match the number you wrote at the end of the exercise on the previous page.

Some of these choices are not easy, but the rest of your personal development program depends on your having a clear picture of your values and priorities. The next step is to define goals or objectives to help you design your life to be consistent with your priorities. Your life will be satisfying to the degree that what you do is consistent with your values.

Setting Goals to Achieve Your Vision

A goal is a statement of what you intend to accomplish. It is an end result, an achievement. A goal is the reason for doing what you do; it is not a task. Tasks are actions taken to meet goals. Many people make lists of things to do, and they may do everything on their lists but still feel that their lives are empty because they have not clarified their values and set appropriate goals. They are people who do a lot but gain little satisfaction from their accomplishments.

Self-empowered people not only accomplish most of what they set out to do, but they also have a clear idea of why they are doing what they do. This helps them enjoy great satisfaction from what they accomplish. If your career value is achievement and promotion, your goals might include completing a business degree or learning more about the opportunities within your organization. If you value a good marriage, your goals might include participating in psychotherapy or counseling or in a couples workshop.

Six Criteria for Defining Goals

It is smart to know your values and set goals to have each of those values satisfied. When you define your goals, you can assure success by making your goals fit six criteria, which can be remembered with the acronym SMARTS:

S **imple and Specific.** Goals must be clearly understood and easy to remember. A vague goal is unlikely to be accomplished. A complex goal must be broken down into simpler goals to ensure success.

M **easurable.** The only way to know if a goal has been achieved is to be able to measure the outcome. Ideally you can use numbers to evaluate your progress and achievement.

A **ttainable.** An impossible goal guarantees failure. To assure success, make your goals realistic and achievable.

R **esults.** State goals by the expected outcome. This helps prevent your defining tasks or steps without clearly identifying what you intend to achieve.

T **ime Limit.** Without a deadline or time limit, it is too easy to procrastinate. A time limit helps you stay focused on your goal. A long-term goal may need to be broken down into several shorter-term goals.

S **hared.** Few achievements are solo performances. You increase your chances for success when you share your goals with others who can support your efforts. Another reason for telling others what you intend to accomplish is that you increase your commitment when you make your goals known to others.

YOUR PERSONAL DEVELOPMENT PROGRAM

Invest whatever amount of time is required to define goals for your higher priority values. This investment of time will pay the dividends of success and self-empowerment. You may have several goals related to one value.

Start by choosing a few of your values and writing at least one goal for each. Later you can complete the job of setting your personal development goals.

Value: _____

Goal: *I will* _____

_____

_____

Value: _____

Goal: *I will* _____

_____

_____

Value: _____

Goal: *I will* _____

_____

_____

Check your goals against the SMARTS criteria. Because most of us have not been taught about setting goals, it is easy to leave something out. Making sure each goal passes the SMARTS test adds to your self-empowerment by increasing your chances for success.

You will probably find that you will accomplish many of your goals without having a definite plan. Once you have a quality goal clearly defined and embedded in your subconscious, you tend to go about achieving it without even being aware that you are doing so.

Self-empowered people, however, don't just assume this will happen. The next step in your personal development program is to design action steps for each goal.

CONTINUED

For each of the goals you have defined, list action steps toward the accomplishment of your goal. List anything that would contribute to the eventual accomplishment. Later you can decide which actions you will take and in what order you will complete the tasks.

Example:

Value: health and physical fitness.

Goal: I will lose 10 pounds during the next 90 days and will maintain my weight at this new level.

Action steps: Read a book on nutrition and exercise, join a health club, exercise three or four days each week for a minimum of 30 minutes each time, switch from ice cream to nonfat frozen yogurt, eat smaller quantities, drink plenty of water each day.

Goal 1 Action steps: _____

_____

_____

Goal 2 Action steps: _____

_____

_____

Goal 3 Action steps: _____

_____

_____

Invest the time to develop action steps for each of your goals to help ensure you live in a way consistent with the values you have identified as being most important to you. This is the best way to guarantee success in all aspects of your life.

Putting time limits on each of the action steps you choose for the goal also will help you succeed. Procrastination is a common problem with goal achievement, and time limits help keep you on track.

Creating Support Systems

It can make a big difference in your personal development program to create a support system for yourself. Self-empowered people know they do not have to accomplish everything alone and that involving others in their lives adds to their enjoyment and empowers them further.

A support system includes those people who help you, who encourage you, who listen to your concerns and troubles, who provide information, who hold you and comfort you, who play with you, and who help you celebrate your successes. Identify who these people are, then share your goals with them and involve them in developing your plans for accomplishment.

IDENTIFY YOUR SUPPORT GROUP

Identify who gives you the following kinds of support and consider how well they do it. Rate them from 1 (poor) to 5 (excellent). You may have more than one person in some categories or you may have none. Think about whom you might seek for this support if the first person you list failed to come through to your satisfaction or if you have no one to list.

Support	Person	Rating	Who Else?
Encouragement			
Assistance			
Comfort			
Information			
Listening			
Challenge			
Fun/Celebration			

If you discover that you depend upon the same person for all kinds of support, consider adding more people to your support group. How would you cope if you lost this one person? How much more support could you enjoy if you allowed more people into your life? How much richer could your life become if you shared it with others?

Rewarding Yourself

A final suggestion for your personal development program is to set up a reward system. Having such a program increases the number of successes in your life and adds to the pleasure of satisfying your values. Sometimes it takes a long time to reach a goal, and it is easy to become discouraged or to lose sight of the eventual satisfaction waiting for you when you finally achieve that long-term goal. Rewards for completing tasks along the way keep you going and provide you with more energy for the quest.

Some of the best rewards are those that please the child who still lives inside you, the little kid who is the primary source of your creativity, enthusiasm, play, intuition, and emotions. It is that little kid who is so easily discouraged or disappointed and who needs the revitalization of frequent rewards.

WHAT DOES YOUR "LITTLE KID" LIKE?

Check (✔) all of the following that appeal to the child inside you. Be spontaneous and playful as you read the list and allow yourself to check any that appeal to you. (Turn off that disapproving parent who lives in there too!)

- ❏ **Having a party**
- ❏ **New clothes**
- ❏ **Surprises**
- ❏ **Food treats**
- ❏ **Watching sports**
- ❏ **Dancing**
- ❏ **Travel**

Have the idea now? While you are in the mood, list other specific rewards that would motivate you. You can list anything you want.

More Fun Stuff I Like:

_____

_____

_____

_____

_____

Now that you have identified what you would enjoy as rewards for your efforts, make definite plans to give one of these to yourself when you complete an action step or when you achieve a goal within a set time limit. Ask others to give you one of these rewards when they see you doing what you have committed to do or to surprise you with a reward if they notice you are becoming discouraged. What a wonderful way to involve others in your personal development program. This idea works and will help you achieve your goals.*

*More help for your personal development program can be found in the following books from Crisp Publications: Developing Self-Esteem by Connie Palladino; Achieving Results by Lorna Riley; Be Your Own Coach by Barbara Braham and Christina Wahl; Finding Your Purpose by Barbara J. Braham; and Successful Self-Management by Paul Timm.

Maintaining Momentum

Becoming a self-empowered person requires that you practice and use the ideas presented in this book. Adult educators note that within 24 hours you will forget up to 75% of what you learned, and two weeks from now you will have forgotten 90%. The human memory greatly resembles a sieve!

Use the following suggestions to help you remember what you have learned and continue with your movement toward self-empowerment:

➤ Review this book tomorrow. Unless you have a photographic memory, you are going to forget some of it, but a review within 24 hours will help you retain much more.

➤ Read the book again within two weeks, and think about your answers to the exercises. Change some if they need changing, and write new goals as you think of them.

➤ Talk with someone about what you learned. The ideas you share will be what you will remember best. There is an old saying that seems to be true: "The best way to learn something is to teach it." When you discuss these ideas with others, you are recording them in your long-term memory.

➤ Commit to reading at least two or three other books listed in this book's footnotes or in the reading list at the end of this book.

➤ Listen to an audiotape or videotape program. Many of the titles in the Crisp Publications collection have accompanying video and audio programs that you can buy or rent to supplement your reading. Other sources listed also offer programs that relate to the topics in this book.

➤ Take a course or seminar relating to these topics.

➤ Review this book again after one month.

➤ Reward yourself for following up.

Personal growth and self-empowerment are much like personal hygiene or exercise: You have to practice the behaviors regularly before they become habits. By using the ideas and techniques regularly—even daily—you will eventually find that you are doing them automatically. Continuing self-empowerment will become a wonderful new habit. We wish you much success!

A P P E N D I X

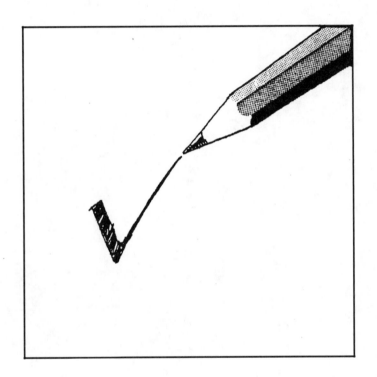

Author's Comments on the Case Studies

Interpersonal Failing Leads to Firing (page 8)

Did you check trust as a missing characteristic? That might be a good guess, but little evidence exists to indicate that trusting others was Robert's difficulty. If you checked interpersonal skills, you correctly identified his most obvious problem.

Robert's experience is a common one. Many talented people fail to achieve their potential because they do not have the skills for dealing with people. Research conducted by the American Management Association revealed that the typical manager spends as much as 80% of the workday in face-to-face interaction. Robert's experience illustrates one of the most common reasons for firing managers: They treat people with disrespect, and they are aggressive and abrasive. Interpersonal skills are necessary for success in almost every endeavor.

Lamenting Life Lost (page 20)

Jack is an example of the many people who go through life allowing events and others to determine how they live. To such people, life seems to be something that happens to them rather than something they determine for themselves. These people often look back and wonder where all the time went and how they managed to get so little pleasure from their lives.

Self-empowered people approach life differently.

In reality, everyone's life is self-determined. Those who are passive in their approach to life, reacting to events and allowing others to set their priorities, are responsible for choosing to live their lives passively. When you are self-determined, you actively identify your own values, wants, and needs; define your own goals; and chart your own path through life.

Expectations and Outcomes (page 23)

The key to Connie's more effective management style is her underlying expectations and attitudes. She expects others to be responsible and dependable. She has positive expectations about life in general, which allow her to be relaxed and free of stress. Her frequent contact with employees indicates she genuinely likes people.

In contrast, Terry expects things to be difficult and believes that success requires hard work. She seems to sweat and strain unnecessarily, causing others around her to feel pressure.

Pat's most obvious characteristic is a negative attitude. He responds spontaneously by seeing only the faults and reasons for not being cooperative. You can imagine how Pat's face looks and the tone of voice he uses when he makes these negative remarks. No wonder people leave his department.

Each of these managers displays different behavior, and it is the behavior that influences others. Each person's behavior is a consequence of underlying expectations and attitudes. If Pat and Terry changed their outlooks, their behaviors also would change.

Seeking Cooperation (page 37)

If you said no to the first two questions, you agree with the authors. Marti should use I-statements and a clear request with each representative to get a better understanding and commitment. She could say, "I need to have your sales report by Wednesday each report period to give me enough time to prepare the summary report for the regional manager. Will you please help me by making sure you get your report to me by then?"

Merely telling the representatives "you need to do this" was not communicating Marti's own wants and needs in a direct way. Her communication style sounds parental and might prompt resentment or rebellion rather than cooperation.

If you suggested that Marti have her boss intercede, that would probably get results. But the sales representatives might feel resentful that she took that approach, and she would not gain the respect that being more self-empowered and negotiating her own agreements would earn.

Delegating or Dumping? (page 63)

Marvin's instructions are specific and clear, but he could improve on all other counts.

Marvin is guilty of a common management mistake. He doesn't seem to understand the difference between delegating and dumping. By assigning specific and somewhat menial tasks to Tony each month, he is ignoring the opportunity to redesign the whole reporting system, which could provide a one-time solution for his problem. He has dumped a boring, routine task on an employee when he could have delegated a challenging responsibility.

Marvin repeats his mistake with Ellen by dumping the undesirable task of lecturing the support staff rather than investigating the problem to discover the root causes. Ellen attempts to suggest that other aspects need to be considered, but she is interrupted by her manager, who apparently assumes that his answers are the only right ones.

You can imagine the conversation between Tony and Ellen after they left Marvin's office. Do you think their respect for their manager may have dropped a notch or two? How do you think they feel about their assignments?

Delegating to Empower (page 70)

Quite an improvement, right? This still is not a perfect delegation, but excellence does not require perfection. With this approach, Tony and Marvin will have a better relationship. Tony will do a better job with this assignment, and the improvement in efficiency will be many times greater than the original approach. Tony has willingly and enthusiastically accepted this responsibility and knows he is accountable for the results. Marvin also has grown in his self-empowerment by having empowered Tony.

One Mistake Leads to Another (page 74)

If you said his mistakes included failing to follow up the delegation in writing or to make sure the follow-up was carried out as agreed—remember the weekly progress report?—you are right. If you said another mistake was confronting Tony in front of his peers, you agree with the authors. An important element in handling the mistakes of others is choosing an appropriate time and place.

A Positive Learning Experience (page 78)

Obviously, this approach takes a few more minutes than scolding Tony in the hallway, but the outcome is well worth the extra time and effort. Tony will have gained respect for Marvin because he handled the situation so skillfully and because he revealed a little of his own imperfections. Tony also will have less fear about accepting new responsibilities and being accountable for his decisions and actions when he knows his boss will handle mistakes in this positive coaching manner. Marvin has added to his self-empowerment by turning a problem into an improvement in his relationship with Tony, and Tony's project is more likely to conclude successfully.*

---

*For additional ideas on improving your coaching skills as part of your self-empowerment growth, read Coaching and Counseling by Marianne Minor, Crisp Publications.

Confronting a Co-Worker (page 89)

Kerry's behavior: failing to complete work on time.

Effects of the behavior: delaying project completion; eroding trust in the relationship; receiving criticism from the manager; placing Liu in the position of either doing more work or suffering the negative consequences of a failed project.

Emotions: frustrated, angry, disappointed, concerned, embarrassed.

Request for change: ask Kerry for a solution; ask Kerry to do the work for which he is responsible; ask Kerry to report to the manager that the project completion will be delayed and to explain why.

Author's Suggested Responses to Exercises

Evaluate Your Trust Level (page 5)

If you checked only numbers 2, 4, 5, and 10, you display an unusual amount of trust in others. People who are trusting typically assume that others are honest and dependable. Trusting people are comfortable sharing problems and feelings with others. People who trust others are people who see themselves as okay, and they see others as okay, too.

The other statements in the list indicate some lack of trust in others' abilities or motivations. Whether the doubt is related to others' dependability, commitment, skills, honesty, attitudes, motivation, or intelligence, the result is the same. When you do not trust, you will limit your self-empowerment and be reluctant to empower others. You will also be reluctant to confide in others or to allow them to be part of your efforts, which means that you will miss opportunities to benefit from their support, assistance and creativity.

What Do You Expect? (page 24)

In each case, if your answer represents your genuine expectation, your actual experience would be likely to turn out as you expected. If you respond to your boss's surprise assignment with pride and pleasure and you expect to do well, you probably will. If you react with dismay or anger and expect to have difficulties, you probably will.

If all you can imagine about accompanying your spouse to the reunion is being bored or uncomfortable with so many strangers, then you will have just the experience you expect.

The third situation is common. Having advance information about someone will prejudice your perception of that person and help to create the relationship you expected. Most people would expect to feel tense with Terry and would probably plan to counsel her about time management. Most would expect conflict with Pat and an ongoing struggle to obtain cooperation. And most would predict a smooth, successful relationship with Connie.

Sure enough, the relationships proceed just as expected.

Communicating Positive Expectations (page 28)

Answers: Numbers 1, 4, 5, 7, and 8 are win-win examples. Numbers 2, 3, 7, 9, and 10 communicate negative expectations of self or others. Numbers 9 and 10 reveal self-defeating expectations.

Clear or Vague? (page 34)

If you marked numbers 3, 5, 7, 8 and 10 as clear communication, you agree with the authors. The others are not clear, for the following reasons:

➤ Number 1 is a passive, negative approach to getting a want satisfied. The person speaking seems to want to go to the movies, but instead asks the others if they don't want to go.

➤ Number 2 comes across as an attack, asking the others to explain their behavior rather than communicating what the speaker wants.

➤ Number 4 is tentative and passive, which allows others to make the decision.

➤ Number 6 asks whether the others are firm in their desire rather than stating what the speaker wants.

➤ Number 9 is passive and tentative, which makes it easy for the other person to say no.

Practice Establishing Agreements (page 39)

Authors' ideas: Bill could offer a higher-quality finished project using the marketing research data. He could say, "My team and I believe that we could improve our projections with some marketing research and we need more time and some additional money for a consulting firm. Will you please approve an extension of three weeks and an additional $3,000?"

Authors' ideas: Lisa could offer to do the same for Jennifer on another occasion. She could say, "Jennifer, I have a date with a great new guy. He is taking me to a social hour, dinner, and a terrific concert, and I would like to leave right at quitting time to get ready. Will you please close out for me, and I'll do the same for you another time?"

Practice Active Listening (page 56)

1. Fed up, frustrated, or annoyed; complaints

2. Frustrated; your report, all those numbers

3. I'm selfish, I don't ask you what you want; hurt, angry

Identify the Real Problem (page 81)

The labels come easily, don't they? Learning to stop judging and attaching negative labels is an important step toward self-empowerment. The self-empowered person makes the extra effort to withhold judgment and to discuss problems with others in a way that communicates respect, even when their behavior is such that most people would disapprove of it.

1. Sally could be described as a snob or hateful or tacky.

   Her actual behavior is making a disparaging remark about Perry's clothing.

2. Jeremy could be described as sloppy, careless, or lazy.

   His actual behavior is submitting reports with omissions and computational errors.

3. Will could be described as a flirt, a male chauvinist pig, or as obnoxious, fresh, or gross.

   His actual behavior is swatting Ann's buttocks and making a sexually suggestive remark. Describing it as sexual harassment would be accurate, but not as helpful in a confrontational discussion as the more factual description.

4. Monica could be described as dictatorial, bossy, or insensitive toward others.

   Her actual behavior is shouting at employees and threatening them.

Recommended Reading

Personal Growth

Briggs, Dorothy Corkille. *Celebrate Your Self.* NY: Doubleday, 1986.

Butler, Pamela E. *Talking to Yourself.* NY: Harper & Row, 1981.

Dyer, Wayne W. *Your Erroneous Zones.* NY: HarperCollins, 1997.

James, Muriel. *It's Never Too Late to Be Happy.* Boston, MA: Addison-Wesley, 1985.

Lloyd, Sam R. *Developing Positive Assertiveness.* Menlo Park, CA: Crisp Publications, 2000.

McKay, Matthew, & Patrick Fanning. *Self-Esteem.* Oakland, CA: New Harbinger, 1987.

McKay, M., M. Davis, & P. Fanning. *Messages: The Communications Skills Book.* Oakland, CA: New Harbinger, 1983.

Relationships

Hendrix, Harville. *Getting the Love You Want.* NY: Harper & Row, 1988.

Paul, Jordan, & Margaret Paul. *Do I Have to Give Up Me to Be Loved by You?* Minneapolis, MN: Compcare, 1983.

Management Skills

Burley-Allen, Madelyn. *Managing Assertively.* NY: John Wiley & Sons, 1981.

Byham, William. *Zapp! The Lightning of Empowerment.* NY: Ballantine Group, 1997.

Gordon, Thomas. *Leader Effectiveness Training.* NY: Bantam Doubleday Dell, 1986.

LeBoeuf, Michael. *The Greatest Management Principle in the World.* NY: Berkeley, 1986.

Lloyd, Sam R. *Leading Teams: The Skills for Success.* Urbandale, IA: American Media, 1998.

Audio Programs

Lloyd, Sam, & Linda Stone. *Win-Win Relationships.* SuccessSystems, Boulder, Colorado, www.trainingforsuccess.com

Tracy, Brian. *The Psychology of Achievement.* Nightingale-Conant.

NOTES

Now Available From

Books•Videos•CD-ROMs•Computer-Based Training Products

If you enjoyed this book, we have great news for you.
There are over 200 books available in the *Fifty-Minute*™ *Series*.
To request a free full-line catalog, contact your local distributor or

Crisp Learning
1200 Hamilton Court
Menlo Park, CA 94025
1-800-442-7477
CrispLearning.com

Subject Areas Include:

Management
Human Resources
Communication Skills
Personal Development
Marketing/Sales
Organizational Development
Customer Service/Quality
Computer Skills
Small Business and Entrepreneurship
Adult Literacy and Learning
Life Planning and Retirement

Self-Empowerment

CRISP WORLDWIDE DISTRIBUTION

English language books are distributed worldwide. Major international distributors include:

ASIA/PACIFIC

Australia/New Zealand: In Learning, PO Box 1051, Springwood QLD, Brisbane, Australia 4127   Tel: 61-7-3-841-2286, Facsimile: 61-7-3-841-1580
ATTN: Messrs. Richard/Robert Gordon

Hong Kong/Mainland China: Crisp Learning Solutions, 18/F Honest Motors Building 9-11 Leighton Rd., Causeway Bay, Hong Kong   Tel: 852-2915-7119, Facsimile: 852-2865-2815 ATTN: Ms. Grace Lee

Indonesia: Pt Lutan Edukasi, Citra Graha, 7th Floor, Suite 701A, Jl. Jend. Gato Subroto Kav. 35-36, Jakarta 12950 Indonesia Tel: 62-21-527-9060/527-9061 Facsimile: 62-21-527-9062 ATTN: Mr. Suwardi Luis

Japan: Phoenix Associates, Believe Mita Bldg., 8th Floor 3-43-16 Shiba, Minato-ku, Tokyo 105-0014, Japan   Tel: 81-3-5427-6231, Facsimile: 81-3-5427-6232
ATTN: Mr. Peter Owans

Malaysia, Philippines, Singapore: Epsys Pte Ltd., 540 Sims Ave #04-01, Sims Avenue Centre, 387603, Singapore   Tel: 65-747-1964, Facsimile: 65-747-0162 ATTN: Mr. Jack Chin

CANADA

Crisp Learning Canada, 60 Briarwood Avenue, Mississauga, ON L5G 3N6 Canada
Tel: 905-274-5678, Facsimile: 905-278-2801 ATTN: Mr. Steve Connolly

EUROPEAN UNION

England: Flex Learning Media, Ltd., 9-15 Hitchin Street,
Baldock, Hertfordshire, SG7 6AL, England
Tel: 44-1-46-289-6000, Facsimile: 44-1-46-289-2417   ATTN: Mr. David Willetts

INDIA

Multi-Media HRD, Pvt. Ltd., National House, Floor 1, 6 Tulloch Road,
Appolo Bunder, Bombay, India 400-039 Tel: 91-22-204-2281,
Facsimile: 91-22-283-6478 ATTN: Messrs. Ajay Aggarwal/ C.L. Aggarwal

SOUTH AMERICA

Mexico: Grupo Editorial Iberoamerica, Nebraska 199, Col. Napoles, 03810 Mexico, D.F. Tel: 525-523-0994, Facsimile: 525-543-1173   ATTN: Señor Nicholas Grepe

SOUTH AFRICA

Corporate: Learning Resources, PO Box 2806, Parklands, Johannesburg 2121, South Africa, Tel: 27-21-531-2923, Facsimile: 27-21-531-2944 ATTN: Mr. Ricky Robinson

MIDDLE EAST

Edutech Middle East, L.L.C., PO Box 52334, Dubai U.A.E.
Tel: 971-4-359-1222, Facsimile: 971-4-359-6500   ATTN: Mr. A.S.F. Karim